HABITUDES®

IMAGES
THAT FORM
LEADERSHIP
HABITS &
ATTITUDES

BY

DR TIM ELMORE

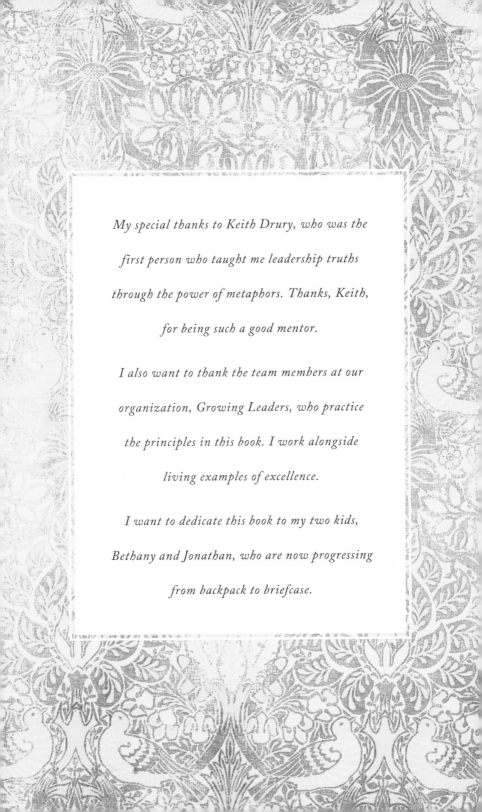

My special thanks to Keith Drury, who was the

first person who taught me leadership truths

through the power of metaphors. Thanks, Keith,

for being such a good mentor.

I also want to thank the team members at our

organization, Growing Leaders, who practice

the principles in this book. I work alongside

living examples of excellence.

I want to dedicate this book to my two kids,

Bethany and Jonathan, who are now progressing

from backpack to briefcase.

PUBLISHED IN ATLANTA, GEORGIA BY GROWING LEADERS, INC. (WWW.GROWINGLEADERS.COM)

ISBN: 978-0-9960783-4-4
PRINTED IN THE UNITED STATES OF AMERICA
LIBRARY OF CONGRESS CATALOGUING-IN-PUBLICATION DATA

TABLE OF CONTENTS

These thirteen images paint a picture of how team members should approach their first job and career. These habits and attitudes will spark growth and rewards at work.

A WORD ABOUT IMAGES

We live in a culture rich with images. You grew up with photos, TV, movies, video, Facebook, MTV, Instagram and DVDs. We can't escape the power of a visual image… and most of us don't want to.

I've learned over my career that most of us are visual learners. We like to see a picture, not just hear a word. Author Leonard Sweet says that images are the language of the 21st century, not words. Some of the best communicators in history taught using the power of the metaphor and image—from Jesus Christ and His parables to Martin Luther King Jr. and his "I Have a Dream" speech during the Civil Rights movement. "The best leaders," writes Tom Peters, "…almost without exception and at every level, are master users of stories and symbols."

Why? Because pictures stick. We remember pictures long after words have left us. When we hear a speech, we often remember the stories from that speech, more than the lines used by the speaker, because they painted a picture inside of us. They communicate far more than mere words. In fact, words are helpful only as they conjure up a picture in our minds. Most of us think in pictures. If I say the word "elephant" to you, you don't picture the letters: e-l-e-p-h-a-n-t. You picture a big gray animal. Pictures are what we file away in our minds. They enable us to store huge volumes of information. There's an old phrase that has stood the test of time: A picture is worth a thousand words. It was while pursuing a college degree in commercial art that I recognized the power of images. Now I get to combine my love of leadership with the power of pictures. I trust they'll impact you profoundly as they have me.

Each image in this book represents a principle you can carry with you the rest of your life. They are truths I wish someone had told me before I entered my career. Most are simple, but each is profound if put into practice. They're all about the soft skills you need to succeed at work. In nationwide surveys, employers continue to reiterate that they're desperately looking for new professionals who possess "soft skills." Hard skills are important—abilities like computing, analyzing and strategic planning—but soft skills differentiate employees who have them: work ethic, great attitudes, teamwork, empathy and communication. For some, the step from a campus to a career feels like a cross-cultural experience. In the same way you feel a little out of place when you travel to a different country, the move from backpack to briefcase may seem like a journey to a foreign land with new values, people, language and customs. The book is designed to be a map to guide you, furnishing pictures to discuss with a community of people. It's part of a series I encourage you to go through in a group. Each picture contains layers of reality, and your discussion can go as deep as you allow it to go. It's a guide for your leadership journey.

Some sociologists describe this generation as EPIC: Experiential, Participatory, Image-rich and Connected. I agree. So each of these books provides you not only with an image, but a handful of discussion questions, a self-assessment and an exercise in which you can participate. Dive in and experience each one of them. My hope is that they become signposts that guide you, warn you, and inform you on your leadership journey.

Dr. Tim Elmore

Coffee Step

EARLY TASKS AREN'T ABOUT SHOWING TALENT BUT EARNING TRUST. BE WILLING TO MAKE THE COFFEE TO EARN A SPOT IN THE ROOM. THE COFFEE "MAKE" LEADS TO THE COFFEE "BREAK."

Kerry Priest served as an entry-level team member after graduating from college. I met her as a young twenty-something, full of potential and eager to learn. She came to a fork in the road, however, in her first month on the job. One of her senior colleagues asked her to make the coffee and bring it to the Monday morning meeting. She confided in me later that she felt a little patronized. "Were they asking me because they assumed this was a suitable task for my skill set? Did they ask me because I'm a female and I wouldn't mind doing this like some males would? Do they not know I have a college degree?" Despite her reservations, Kerry swallowed her pride and got the coffee. Today, she's so glad she did.

It was while Kerry was getting the coffee she recognized an important truth about influence. Getting the coffee didn't have to be seen as a demeaning step in her early career. She could actually leverage it as an advantage. She discovered if she was willing to get the coffee for her colleagues, it actually got her in the room where the meeting took place. Executives began to get to know her and appreciate her. Her face became familiar. Soon, she humbly offered a suggestion or idea in the conversation. Eventually, some in the room were asking her opinion about the issue they were discussing. Ultimately, it became a natural step to invite her to be part of the meeting, even as a young twenty-something. But her first step…was a coffee step. It had nothing to do with proving how gifted or brilliant or savvy she was. She discovered that early tasks on a job are about earning trust more than displaying talent.

As people enter their career, they realize something if they are observant. They'll find that if they are willing to "lean in" to colleagues—to serve them in ways that perhaps others are not willing to serve—it opens the door for greater opportunities. I hired Ben right out of college years ago. He served in a long line of highly gifted interns in our office. When his internship was over, however, we didn't want it to end.

Why? Ben literally practiced this principle. While so many others were trying to prove how smart they were—Ben got the coffee for everyone. Early on, when someone from our executive team asked him to do a Starbucks run, he smiled and said he'd be glad to. From that point on, Ben did the asking. He'd inquire every morning if we wanted some coffee to get the day started. He would bring it to the team with a smile, even laughter, and always with a great attitude. When we offered him a full-time position, he inquired why he was asked instead of the other interns. We told him it was a quality he demonstrated as he got the coffee. We knew he was smart and gifted, but more importantly we could see someone who was willing to roll up his sleeves and do whatever needed to be done, large or small. It was the coffee step that sold us.

It's Not Just About Coffee

I believe this is an early step in almost everyone's leadership journey. With rare exceptions, leaders demonstrate the ability to check their ego at the door, and do what others are unwilling to do, to get in the room. They become consumed with "adding value" not extracting value, salary, benefits or perks. Along the way, they discover the *Law of Reciprocals*. What is generously given...frequently comes back to them. Gestures are reciprocated. Centuries ago, King Solomon wrote a Proverb: "Cast your bread upon the waters, and it will return to you after many days." Simply put, what you toss out to others will boomerang back to you—good or bad.

When someone demonstrates they are willing to do whatever it takes to help the cause, others tend to find ways to open doors for them. This means, however, you often start very small. Consider for a moment some of the most notable celebrities in our culture over the last ten years or so. Many of them learned this lesson—there is no job too small to get your foot in the door. For instance, did you know...

- Johnny Depp's first job...was an over-the-phone pen salesman?
- Simon Cowell's first job...was a mailroom clerk?
- Sandra Bullock's first job...was as a bartender?
- Lady Gaga's first job...was a waitress?
- Brad Pitt...dressed up like a chicken for a restaurant chain?
- Kelly Clarkson...sold Kirby Vacuum Cleaners?
- Matthew McConaughey...actually shoveled chicken manure?

May I talk straight with you? The reason we positioned this "image" first is because so many young job candidates stumble here. Young adults (ages 18-28) continue to be the most unemployed demographic in our country. While this is often true of any young generation, it's especially true today. One nationwide survey found that companies who employ recent graduates could not find enough candidates to fill their positions. Half of their job openings went unfilled because potential employees were unprepared to do the job. In other words, the jobs were ready, but the kids weren't. Condoleezza Rice and Joel Klein released a report saying that 75 percent of teens in America are not even qualified for the military due to obesity, criminal records, or failure to graduate.[1] Over the last five years, Monster. com reported the majority of students were moving back home after college. They felt unready to enter the world. The bottom line? The problem lies in one of two places:

1. CANDIDATES WERE UNABLE TO TAKE THE JOB. (THEY'RE NOT PREPARED)
2. CANDIDATES WERE UNWILLING TO TAKE THE JOB. (THEY'RE NOT HUNGRY)

In my mind, both are a tragedy. More and more, employers across America tell me they are hearing young team members say:

"This job is beneath me."

No doubt, job seekers want meaningful work right out of college. They think: *I didn't pay all this tuition…to push papers.* It's understandable. According to Alexandria Levit, however, it's also important to recognize, we all must "pay our dues," even if we hate that line. She writes, "…a 'dues-paying' structure has remained in place, it's just more difficult to notice. Previously, it was making photocopies, sweeping the floor and getting coffee. I don't think that occurs as much anymore, but you have to be in the trenches a little while to see how the organization operates."[2]

Just remember this: it does not matter if you start at the bottom of the ladder—as long as you are on the right ladder. Just be sure you've chosen an organization you admire; be sure it's a cause you believe in. Then…make the coffee.

Nothing will stop you from progress faster than a sense of entitlement. This is simply the assumption that you deserve more or better rewards than you're getting. Better positions. Better pay. Better perks. Better placement in the office. While these may be true, the best way to get them is not to make a *complaint*…but to make the *coffee*. I know it sounds like a paradox…but you'll be amazed at how you'll earn influence by focusing on what you can give, instead of what you can get.

My friend Kevin hired the cleaners for his office complex. When he interviewed candidates he would underscore the importance of their *integrity* and their *attention to detail*. He repeated the importance of these two qualities...then, he would pay them to try their skills at it for a week, on a trial basis.

Most would proceed to clean the office exactly as they did so many others. They had no idea it was actually a challenge to see if they'd listened to Kevin's priorities. You see, Kevin would stash $1.78 in coins inside the sofa cushions in his office. He knew that if they returned the entire amount, they had cleaned the room in a detailed way and were honest enough to return the exact amount he knew was there.

Sadly, Kevin had to interview several candidates before he found an honest and detailed cleaner worthy of the job. It was a test.

Why not take this "Coffee Step" principle as a challenge yourself? What if you found ways you could offer to take on projects others cannot or will not do?

As a kid, Don Hahn loved Disney films and Disneyland. His family moved to Burbank when he was in high school and he'd visit the theme park, memorizing all the lines in all the rides. When he was twenty, a Disney employee who attended the same church told Don he had a summer job for anyone who's willing to do grunt work. The job was working in the "morgue" which is the basement where all the past artwork is stored. Don interviewed and got it. It was far from glitzy or glamorous. He worked unnoticed for months. After college, he got hired back because he was willing to work for an assistant director, Woolie Reitherman. Don acknowledged, "One of my earliest jobs was to get the coffee for Mr. Reitherman, take notes and clean his Moviola screen. But this got me in the room as they were working on animated films like *The Rescuers* and *The Fox and the Hound*." The rest, as they say, is history.

This was the exposure Don needed. And, it paid off.

Over time, Don rose to a place of influence, becoming both a producer and director. I bet you've seen his work. Don Hahn is credited with producing some of the most successful animated films in recent history including *The Lion King* and *Beauty and the Beast*, the first animated film to be nominated for an Oscar for *Best Picture*. He's played a key role in dozens of other popular Disney projects and currently is the Executive Producer of the *Disneynature* films. What's more, Don owns his own film production company, Stone Circle Pictures. He's now able to write his own ticket in the industry.

It's important to remember, however…it all began with a coffee step.

REFLECT AND RESPOND

1. Have you ever seen a team member go out of their way to serve others in even small and detailed ways?

_____

_____

2. What makes this hard?

_____

_____

3. What's the wildest act of service you've offered at work?

_____

_____

SELF ASSESSMENT

List the top two places you find it difficult to practice this "coffee step" principle. Now, evaluate yourself on why it is so challenging in those situations. Circle your response.

Why is it difficult to "make the coffee:"

    1. Pride – I don't like the idea of feeling lower than others.

    2. Blind spots – I just don't see opportunities to serve like this.

    3. Laziness – I would but I am exhausted just getting my work done.

    4. Apathy – I guess I don't care enough to do the extra acts of kindness.

    5. Other: _____

What could you do to overcome this difficulty and see "coffee step" as an opportunity?

_____

_____

EXERCISE

From your responses above, determine one situation that you could take initiative and see the coffee step as an opportunity instead of a penalty. To make it intriguing, choose a task you would normally never dream of doing. Jot down your plan and later, jot down what you did and how others responded. What did you learn?

IMAGE TWO
[Crockpots and Microwaves]

Crockpots and Microwaves

YOUR PATH TO THE GOAL WILL LIKELY TAKE LONGER THAN YOU ASSUMED NECESSARY. YOU'RE IN A CROCKPOT. YOU MUST BE WILLING TO WAIT TO BE GREAT.

Harlan wondered if he'd just been in too much of a hurry his whole life. He was five when his daddy died, and at fourteen, he dropped out of Greenwood School to start making money. He tried odd jobs for the next several years:

- He tried various tasks as a farm hand in Indiana—and hated it.
- He tried being a streetcar conductor, but it just didn't suit him.
- At sixteen, he lied about his age to join the Army, but quit after one year.
- Afterward, he headed for Alabama and tried to be a blacksmith. He failed.
- He got hired as a fireman with Southern Railroad, but it didn't pan out.

Then, the Great Depression hit in 1929. While he was out job hunting, his young wife gave away all their possessions and went home to live with her parents. Young Harlan had wanted to get started on his career early but never dreamed finding his niche would be so challenging. The good news is—he remained determined to find a place where he was gifted and passionate about working:

- He later tried selling insurance, but that didn't work out either.
- Then, he tried selling tires. Nope. It wasn't for him.
- Then, he tried running a Ferry Boat. Not a fit.
- Then, he tried managing a few gas stations. No stint lasted long.

Harlan's exploration began to narrow, having scratched off jobs that didn't fit him. Finally, after years of working and waiting—he found work that could be his career. He became the chief cook at a restaurant in Corbin. He liked it, and the customers seemed to like him. He flourished until the freeway bypass was moved and business dropped. The café closed. It was then…his expected life span ran out. It was time to retire.

His first social security check was in his mailbox.

Although Harlan felt he was just getting started, the government had sent him a check that basically said its time to stop. It turned out to be a wake up call. He decided to do something crazy by investing that $105 check to start a business doing the one thing he really liked—preparing food. He picked up a recipe and started cooking chicken. It worked. Harlan Sanders is the one you know as Colonel Sanders, and his recipe was for *Kentucky Fried Chicken*. His career took off. He flourished for years. He later sold the restaurant chain to investors for two million dollars when he was 74. He died a wealthy man in 1980, at 90 years old. Wow. Better late than never, right?

I don't know about you, but this story gives me hope. I think if Harlan could return to teach us about our careers, he'd share two lessons. First, it's never too late to rethink your journey, and second…you've got to stick to it. Success will likely take longer than you think it will.

We Live in a Microwave World

I think I know why I admire Colonel Sanders so much. I don't like to wait or work that long to succeed. I give up much too easily. I'm tempted to quit if a project doesn't work after a couple of attempts. In fact, this is a picture of our world today. Thanks to the conveniences of technology, we prefer life fast and easy: high speed Internet access, Instagram, ATM's, fast food, instant messaging…you name it. Let's face it. We live in a microwave world, and we are pacing in front of it, complaining how long the food is taking to cook! (Just kidding on that one). Take a look at the columns below. They remind us of the unintended consequences of our high-tech world:

Today's SCENE Shapes Us:

Our World Is Full Of:	Consequently, We Can Assume:
S – Speed	Slow is bad.
C – Convenience	Hard is bad.
E – Entertainment	Boring is bad.
N – Nurture	Risk is bad.
E – Entitlement	Labor is bad.

Since our world is marked by instant technology, we can tend to assume that slow is bad. We like to avoid anything that takes too long. In addition, our world is full of *conveniences*. We love the amenities of our modern lifestyle. But if we grow up in this world, we can shun anything that's hard. Further, *entertainment* is everywhere. We migrate to our smart phone where external stimuli keeps us amused.

This conditions us to not handle boredom well. And how about nurture? Millions of parents nurture their children, but with too much, risk can be a foreign concept and kids may avoid it. Finally, if we grow up in an environment where so many things are given to us, we can feel entitled: "I deserve this." The unintended consequence? We don't like labor.

You're in a Crockpot

You know the difference between crockpots and microwave ovens. I was a teenager when microwaves were first introduced on the market. We all marveled at how you could cook a meal in minutes, rather than hours. A hot dog took about a minute and a half. Popcorn was no longer a hassle to make. It was all fast and convenient.

Until that time, those who did the cooking did it conventionally, using stoves, ovens and very often, a crockpot. You had to start the process much earlier, and preparation was seldom quick and easy. When my mom used our crockpot, she'd fill it with a stew, including meat, vegetables, potatoes and seasoning. Then—she'd let it sit there for hours, all afternoon. When it was time for dinner, however, it was all worth it. The stew that came out of that crockpot was absolutely delicious. Simmering hot, the roast could be easily pulled apart and would almost melt in your mouth. The potatoes were soft and tasty, as were the veggies. You could tell it was slow roasted. It was so much better than what you got out of a microwave oven after a few minutes. In fact, a microwave meal often grows cold and tough quickly after heating.

So it is with most of our careers. It's a slow roast where we're seasoned by experience, and we accumulate wisdom along the way. It rarely happens overnight, no matter how smart we are. In fact, we often hear about "overnight successes" on reality TV shows, like *American Idol*, or *Survivor* or *The Voice*. But in reality, overnight success is very rare. We need to allow time for our careers to evolve. But it's hard.

I have an attorney friend who interviewed a recent college grad for a job. During the job interview, the young lady smiled and predicted: *"I'm going to have your job in two years."* My friend smiled back, realizing she had no idea what she was talking about, nor how cocky she sounded. He ushered her to the door and dismissed her. Sadly, she left clueless and jobless, assuming her rise to the top was a *sprint* not a *marathon*.

We live in a generation of highlight reels—where we watch the greatest moments of a game between two sports teams, but not the hours of practice the athletes invested in preparation. We admire them and want to be like Lebron James, Albert Pujols, Serena Williams or Peyton Manning—but we often forget they were prepared in a crockpot. Their careers were years in the making, even though they're tremendously gifted.

None of them won a championship right away. Glued to ESPN, we secretly wish we could do what those superstars do, but most of us wouldn't want to do what they did to get there. It was years of private, not so glitzy practice.

Consider These Truths...

1. When it comes to our happiness, life is pretty much about managing expectations.
   We're able to be more patient when we embrace realistic expectations about life.

2. As important as the goal we wait for is the growth we must experience as we wait.
   Our supervisors know our maturity takes time to develop. We're a work in progress.

3. Just like a farmer anticipates a harvest, so our careers require work and waiting.
   When farmers plant seed, they know crops take time—but it's worth the wait.

4. We rarely become disillusioned unless we're first "illusioned."
   We must fight illusions about how quickly or easily things should work out.

The Marshmallow Test

Over 40 years ago, psychologist and Stanford University professor Walter Mischel did a series of studies on delayed gratification in children. A child was brought into a room and given a treat—usually a marshmallow. The child was told that the adult would leave for about 15 minutes and then come back. If the child did not eat the treat, they would be given a second one. If the child did eat the treat, it would be the only treat he received. The follow-up studies showed amazing results. The kids who were able to wait for the second treat had higher SAT scores as teens, better educational attainment, better body mass indexes and did better with other qualities of life. Years later, their careers had actually gone better. Waiting is a soft skill…but it's very tangible.

My Six Realistic Expectations:

1. Life is difficult.
2. Control is a myth.
3. It's not about me.
4. Things take time and will change.
5. No one can make me happy.
6. I must live with the end in mind.

The truth is, our careers are a lot like fishing. We must always be ready to seize each opportunity, but preparation and patience are required. Napoleon Hill said, "Patience, persistence and perspiration make an unbeatable combination for success."

This likely means I've gotta spend a little time in the crockpot.

Reflect and Respond

1. Can you identify other ways the metaphors of a microwave oven and a crockpot illustrate the realities we face in our lives?

_____

_____

_____

2. Do you struggle with waiting on what you want? How do you deal with impatience in yourself?

_____

_____

_____

3. In what area do you currently find it difficult to wait for progress or results? What's the healthiest way you can handle a slow-moving job or career?

_____

_____

_____

Self Assessment

Based on your answer to Question 3 above, evaluate yourself on the following four categories. Give yourself a score between 1 and 10, based on your attitude:

Four Keys to Your Career:

1. Realism: Draw a realistic line for expectations. (Where's your contentment line?)
   I'm discontent   1   2   3   4   5   6   7   8   9   10   I'm content

2. Adaptability: Be flexible (We emotionally calibrate based on what we calculate)
   I'm inflexible   1   2   3   4   5   6   7   8   9   10   I'm flexible

3. Progress: Make sure you're producing results of some kind. (Production is key)
   I don't see progress   1   2   3   4   5   6   7   8   9   10   I produce results

4. Balance: Don't surrender your ultimate hopes, but focus on your work today.
   I have imbalanced focus   1   2   3   4   5   6   7   8   9   10   I have balanced focus

"Never cut a tree down in the wintertime. Never make a negative decision in the low time. Never make your most important decisions when you are in your worst moods. Wait. Be patient. The storm will pass. The spring will come."
– Robert H. Schuller

Choose one situation in which you find it difficult to wait. It could be on your job or in your personal life. Discipline yourself to focus on the *controllables* you can influence, not on the *uncontrollables* you cannot. Make a plan for the steps you'll take this week to work while you wait. Discuss with colleagues how you did.

Early Birds or Mocking Birds

EVERY WORKPLACE HAS TWO BIRDS—MOCKINGBIRDS MERELY IMITATE OTHERS; EARLY BIRDS INITIATE AND SET THE PACE. ASK FOR THE OFFICE KEY.

This idea was sparked by a young team member I hired years ago. He joined our team with a group of five other recent college graduates for a year-long apprenticeship. I could tell they were all committed to do a great job as each dressed professionally, brought a note pad to meetings, and asked lots of questions. This one team member stood out, however, because he was a bit more mature than the others. After being on the job for a couple of weeks, he asked me a very interesting question.

"Could I have a key to the offices?" He inquired.

"Excuse me?" I replied. I thought I misunderstood him.

"I'm not trying to brown nose anyone," he went on. "But I can tell I'm gonna need to get here early to get these projects done with excellence and have time to help out other team members." He paused. "I realize I'm asking a lot for a twenty-two year old team member, but I'd like to get started on my work early and I may have to stay late. I don't want to assume others will be here late, too. I could do this if I had a set of keys."

What I loved about our interaction was I could tell he wasn't trying to impress me. And his goal wasn't to show anyone else up. He sincerely wanted to come in early…not just follow the crowd every morning. He had his own standard for performance, and it was higher than the average person.

A DIFFERENT KIND OF BIRD

This is a picture illustrating a principle I learned over thirty years ago working for Dr. John C. Maxwell. As I watched the incredible team he had put together, I quickly recognized people could be divided into two groups:

1. MOCKINGBIRDS: THOSE WHO DISCOVER WHAT'S EXPECTED AND PURSUE THOSE GOALS. THEY FOLLOW INSTRUCTIONS WELL AND DO EXACTLY AS THEY ARE TOLD.

2. EARLY BIRDS: THOSE WHO SET THE PACE FOR EVERYONE RAISING THE BAR THROUGH THEIR WORK. THEY NOT ONLY FINISH TASKS, BUT TAKE PROJECTS TO A HIGHER LEVEL.

Please understand—there's nothing wrong with Mockingbirds. There are times when your best response is to simply accomplish what your supervisor asks you to do. There are days when you need to simply go with the flow and imitate the rest of the team, especially if you aren't exactly clear on all the details. At other times, however, it is refreshing to an employer when team members catch the gist of a project and do some thinking on their own. Understanding the intent of the task, they're able to give it time, effort and creativity that supervisors cannot. I love it when this happens.

THE FIGHT OF THE CENTURY

In 1921, David Sarnoff approached his manager at RCA. He knew it was a long shot, but he knew revenue was priority one and he had an idea he felt would help their sales really take off. The problem was, he was young, inexperienced and just one paid-grade above an intern.

A boxing match was about to take place between American champ Jack Dempsey and the French boxer Georges Carpentier. Both men were legends. It would be the fight of the century. And 23 year-old David Sarnoff believed RCA should broadcast the fight over the radio. This had never been done before—and it seemed absurd to most. Radio was for classical music and communication in those days, not for sports programs, and few people had radios in their homes. The RCA executives turned Sarnoff down.

But he knew he had a good idea. He approached his boss two more times, and finally was given the go-ahead. However, the project would be done at his own risk…and on his own dime. RCA would give him no money and no staff.

Fortunately for the world, all David Sarnoff needed was permission to try. He borrowed a military radio transmitter and asked a friend of a friend who had a good voice to "call" the match. Then he contacted RCA salesmen he knew and begged them to place radios in all manner of public places—bars, town halls, churches and restaurants.

It worked. Three hundred thousand people heard the fight, and suddenly everyone wanted a radio. By spring of 1922, radio companies were broadcasting news, sports, and music to households all over the country. As David predicted, sales increased and by 1930, David was president of RCA. His idea had transformed the radio industry.

My friend David Salyers is the co-author of the book, *Remarkable*. Each year, I ask David to meet with our newest team members and talk to them about their careers. He always shares two triangles, representing two approaches to preparing for a career:

Traditional Approach   Transformational Approach

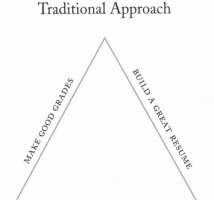 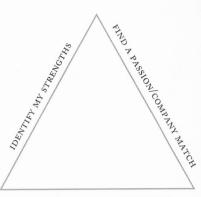

In the *traditional approach*—you work on your GPA, you get involved with activities you believe will look good on the resume, and you interview for jobs you feel will pay you the maximum amount you can get. It's really all about you. Your focus is on what value you can extract once you graduate.

In the *transformational approach*—you seek to identify what value you can add to an organization, by identifying your greatest strengths and passions. You seek out a company that aligns with who you are, not that pays the most. Your focus is primarily on adding value not gaining value. When you approach life this way, you move from *Mockingbird* (acting like everyone else) to *Early Bird* (you stand out from others). Ironically, I have found that money naturally follows the Early Bird.

But that's not all that follows. There are many advantages to playing the role of Early Bird. It's like the classic "first-move advantage" in chess. Since 1851, chess players and theorists generally agree on the inherent advantage of moving first in a match. The statistics show that the first player consistently wins slightly more than the opposition. Consider the kinds of benefits that follow the Early Bird in business:

- You are perceived as the leader – Just think Coca Cola vs. other soft drinks.

- You get noticed and remembered – Just think Kleenex vs. other tissue brands.

- You get to set the pace for others – Just think Amazon vs. other book sellers.

People remember those who go first more than those who follow them. For example, who's the first man to walk on the moon? Most know it was Neil Armstrong. Do you know who was second? Few remember Buzz Aldrin. Roger Bannister is the first man to run a mile in under four minutes. Few know John Landy's name who did it two months later. The Wright Brothers are credited with building the first working airplane, but most don't know the many who flew just weeks later. *We remember the Early Bird.*

What If...

I am sure you've heard the phrase: "The Early Bird gets the worm." It simply means that when you're out in front of others, you tend to be the one who reaps a harvest.

Have you ever heard a Mockingbird? It got its name because it literally can imitate (or mock) the sounds of other birds. In fact, they've been known to mimic the sound of other bird songs, a power lawn mower or even a jackhammer! Amusing. You can see, however, that they get their cues from the voices of others. They are imitators.

What if you became the pacesetter for others? What if you stopped *imitating* and started *initiating*? This will require you to do more than get an idea. You must step out, take a risk and do something. Johann Wolfgang Von Goethe said, "Knowing is not enough; we must apply. Wishing is not enough; we must do." Ivern Ball summarized it this way, "Knowledge is power, but enthusiasm pulls the switch."

So, starting tomorrow, what if you…

- Finished your work early and looked around for ways to help others?
- Took initiative on team projects and volunteered to put in extra effort?
- Determined you'd meet higher standards on your current projects?
- Came in early to your workplace and sought to add value to teammates?
- Made creativity not just compliance your goal at work?

Bill Treasurer made a concept popular among corporate leaders then wrote a book about it. It's called, *Leaders Open Doors.* He actually came up with the concept when his young son came home from his first day of school. When Bill asked his little boy how his day went, his son told him it was great—the teacher had asked him to be the leader for his class. *Wow*, Bill thought. *That's quite a challenge on the first day.* So, he decided to ask his son just what that meant to a five-year-old.

His son beamed and said, "I get to open the doors for everyone else."

That's it, he thought. Wisdom had just surfaced from a kindergarten student. Leaders open doors for others. They pave the way for teammates to make progress. They serve. They create opportunity. They make sure everyone else gets what they need, and after holding the "door" for others to walk through first, leaders may just eat lunch last.

It's the paradox of the Early Bird. Are you OK with that?

Reflect and Respond

1. Discuss some reasons why it's much safer for young employees to play the role of "mockingbird" instead of "early bird."

_____

_____

2. Can you name a time when you set the pace for others? What happened?

_____

_____

3. What would be the downsides if everyone simply was a mockingbird?

_____

_____

Self Assessment

Evaluate yourself on the following three categories, placing an "X" on the dotted line, where you believe it most accurately describes your style:

What's Your Natural Response?

1. When given a new assignment by your supervisor, what's your first reaction?
   Compliance --- Creativity

2. When the organization's goals are not being met, what do you tend to do?
   Take shelter --- Take a risk

3. When unsure about what to do next during the day, what's your default mode:
   Imitate --- Initiate

Neither extreme is always right or wrong…but discuss your natural style.

Exercise

This next week, choose one specific area of your job and be an "Early Bird." Even if it feels fake, choose to get an early start on your day, or to set the pace for others with your work ethic or creativity. Once you choose the area, practice "Early Bird" characteristics every day for one entire week. Don't do it to be noticed, or "liked" or tweeted about. No social media is necessary. Do it under the radar, but daily apply the ideas in this chapter. After a week, talk over the outcomes. Did anyone benefit?

Trains and Tracks

IT WOULD BE EASY TO ASSUME A TRAIN TRACK PREVENTS A TRAIN FROM
MOVING FREELY. IT'S JUST THE OPPOSITE. SYSTEMS ARE YOUR BEST WAY TO
MAKE PROGRESS.

Greg served on our team as a college student. He was creative, spontaneous and
very gifted. I recognized right away I would need to lead him differently than
other young team members, but we hit an impasse within his first three months
on the job.

- We asked each team member to dress "business casual," but Greg wanted to
  wear jeans, flip flops and shirts that could sport his tattoos.

- We asked everyone to do a "time audit" for a week to see where they spent
  their hours and perhaps improve on time management. He felt it was punitive.

- We asked each person to use our customer relationship management system
  so we could track conversations and progress. He called it "red tape."

When Greg refused to follow through on these policies, I met with him to find out
why. His response was predictable. He felt they were unnecessary confinements,
hindering him from being who he really was. It was just too much "red tape" to
wade through. He felt our policies were preventing us from really achieving our
mission. In fact, he said they were "suffocating" to his creativity.

I liked Greg and believed in his potential, so instead of debating the policies, I
tried a little experiment with him. For another month, I let him dress how he
wanted, bypass the time audit and neglect using the CRM system. In short, I let
him "wing it."

The results were vivid.

Two board members happened to visit our office unannounced, saw Greg's
personal dress code and were a bit shocked. Greg could tell it was awkward. In
addition, a university dean (from one of our partner schools) stopped by to talk
over a purchase.

Greg began the meeting, but the dean asked to meet with someone else who had some decision-making authority. Due to Greg's demeanor, the dean didn't take him seriously. Further, Greg's work began falling behind his colleagues. He didn't meet his goals, and by month's end, he was failing miserably. When we talked, he realized he wasn't managing his hours well at all. A time audit would've helped immensely. Everyone else had done one…and outperformed him easily. Finally, during a phone conversation with a partner school, Greg consistently had to put the person on hold to ask a teammate the details of last year's transaction. Greg's teammate pointed out that all those details were on our customer relations management system. Hmmm. If Greg had been using it, he would have known and not had to interrupt anyone.

In short, Greg soon discovered that all of our policies actually had some merit to them. They weren't simply "red tape" to wade through. There was a method to the madness.

LOCOMOTIVES AND RAILROAD TRACKS

Greg learned this *Habitude* the hard way. He discovered that we didn't love "policies" any more than he did. No one on our team wanted to stifle creativity or invent more rules just for the sake of rules. We had simply created systems that helped us get our work done more efficiently.

Imagine a locomotive engineer stopping his train at a station along his route and secretly telling the local residents that he was planning a rebellion. (I know it sounds wild, but imagine this scenario for a moment.) He was fed up with the confinements the railroad company had given him, and he was about to buck the system. After hearing him complain about how he'd been hindered from really making progress in his career, his listeners asked him, "What do you plan to do?"

"I plan to jump the tracks tomorrow morning, and take off into the mountains," he said.

When everyone gasped in astonishment, he continued. "Yep. I'm tired of being limited to these narrow railroad tracks. I'm headed for the hills to show everyone what I can do, where I can take this train, and how fast I can get there."

"Wait," one person replied. "You mean to tell us that you're no longer going to keep the train on the railroad tracks?"

"That's right, partner. You're about to see what real freedom looks like."

Hmmm. This little imaginary scene is preposterous, isn't it? It's the stuff you might see in a cartoon, but no person in his right mind would ever assume taking a train off the tracks would actually improve his progress. Right?

But have you ever paused to consider why?

While they don't allow trains to go anywhere they want, railroad tracks actually help the engineer get to the right destinations more swiftly and without accident. They are a system to enable a train to reach its goal the best way possible. They don't hinder, they help. They harness speed, strength, and velocity.

SYSTEMS ARE YOUR FRIEND

So it is with systems at work. They may seem unnecessary at first, but most of them have a legitimate reason for existence. They harness energy. H. Jackson Brown, Jr. said, "Talent without discipline is like an octopus on roller skates. There's plenty of movement, but you never know if it's going to be forward, backwards, or sideways."

As a new team member, there's nothing wrong with asking "why" some system is in place. It may be antiquated and could be improved upon. In the end, however, every employee discovers they need systems to get things done effectively.

- Systems allow you to place information in a compartment, so you can use your conscious mind for new or non-repeatable tasks. They alleviate mental energy. You don't have to remember as much. Work moves from conscious to sub-conscious mind.

- Systems allow you to speed up a series of tasks, because they are "files for conduct" on the job. They allow you to accelerate a sequence of actions. You can move more quickly and get more done.

- Systems actually foster creativity. Instead of confining your mind, they free up mental space to venture out into the unknown. A system usually exists in the left hemisphere of your brain, so your right hemisphere can dream.

IN SHORT, SYSTEMS...

- IMPROVE RESULTS
- DEEPEN COLLABORATION
- ACCELERATE SPEED
- EXPAND YOUR ABILITY TO SCALE
- CREATE BEHAVIOR
- FOSTER THE ORGANIZATION'S CULTURE

Systems are simply an organization's approach to getting things done. Good ones enable staff to move repeated tasks to an efficient sub-conscious behavior. Bad ones fail to do this. They don't improve results. It's been said that 80% of an organization's problems are not "people problems" but systems problems. The systems don't enable people to perform at their best. The fact is, the system each company adopts will impact what staff members do. Just like railroad tracks either take a train toward or away from its intended destination, a good system improves progress; a bad system impedes progress. The key is for you to identify and embrace good ones.

These can be as simple as...

- A daily or weekly "to do" list, marked in order of priority.
- A customer relationship management system to track interactions.
- A weekly "stand up" meeting where staff hold each other accountable for tasks.
- A file for content, regular events, repeatable tasks or emails.
- A plan for generating leads for new customers or partners.

GETTING STARTED ON A SYSTEM-BASED WORK STYLE

I recommend a handful of repeatable practices for you as a young leader:

1. EACH AFTERNOON, CHOOSE YOUR THREE "BIG ROCKS" FOR THE NEXT DAY.
This is based on another *Habitude*, called *"Big Rocks First."* It applies the wisdom of identifying your three most important, most productive tasks and tending to them first. The principle reminds us: the top 20% of your priorities provide you with 80% of the results you're after. Good systems avoid easy things first...and do first things first.

2. CREATE A PROCESS-ORIENTED APPROACH TO MANAGE WORKFLOW.
The more you use a system the more options you have. Choose a plan that's:

- Simple – Anyone can grasp the system. It's easy to remember.
- Structured – Anyone can practice the system thanks to repeatable steps.
- Scalable – Anyone can learn and later multiply the system in others.
- Successful – Since they're repeatable and transferable, you experience success.

3. DO YOUR WORK IN BLOCKS.
If possible, plan the types of tasks you do by similarity. For example, I do all my admin work in the morning; people work around midday and planning meetings in the afternoon. By blocking my people and non-people time I can emotionally prepare for each type of brain-work. Admin work, people time, and planning tasks are my big three.

4. MAXIMIZE INTERRUPTIONS.
Yes, you read that right. Most people try to minimize their interruptions. Instead, keep a stack of sticky notes or 3X5 note cards nearby. On the top of each one, write down a person's name who you know will interrupt you sometime today.

Next time the person comes over to ask, "Do you have a minute?" say yes, and also talk about the few things you've come up with that are on your list for them. Resist the urge to interrupt them when you think of something. Simply add it to the list. Imagine the time you'd save if people would do this for you.

As you begin your career, you may find yourself wondering why all the "systems" are in place at work. They'll often seem like too much red tape. Just remember there was a reason for each one. They foster the discipline to get things done. Zig Ziglar reminds us: "It was character that got us out of bed, commitment that moved us into action, and discipline that enabled us to follow through."

REFLECT AND RESPOND

1. Talk over both the positives and negatives of having systems.
_____
_____

2. Give an example when you created a system that enabled you to reach a goal.
_____
_____

3. What is one area you definitely need to adopt a system for in your work?
_____
_____

SELF ASSESSMENT

Evaluate your work habits. Choose two common tasks you could improve upon if you had a more effective system in place. Identify what prevents you from using a system:

1. Task: _____

What prevents you from a better system:
- I don't fully understand the task   • I don't have time; too much to do
- I'm not good at creating systems   • Other: _____

2. Task: _____

What prevents you from a better system:
- I don't fully understand the task   • I don't have time; too much to do
- I'm not good at creating systems   • Other: _____

EXERCISE

Now select one of those tasks above and plan the steps you'll take to overcome your current mode of operation. Do what you need to do to put a system in place that will improve performance and speed. Discuss what you did and how it impacted your work.

HARD
BALL

SOFT
BALL

220

200

180

160

140

120

100

80

130

FIRM
BALL

THREAD

100

80

60

40

BALL

THRE

220

200

180

160

140

120

100

80

100

80

60

40

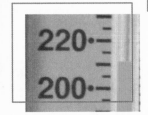

212 Degrees

AT 211 DEGREES, WATER IS A VERY HOT LIQUID. AT 212 DEGREES, IT BECOMES STEAM THAT CAN POWER A LOCOMOTIVE. IT'S THAT LITTLE EXTRA THAT DIFFERENTIATES WORKERS.

Thomas A. Edison is known as the greatest inventor America has ever produced. He's most remembered for the phonograph, for launching motion pictures, and for creating the incandescent light bulb. In the end, he patented over a thousand inventions. Even when he was alive, he was a folk hero. Over 50,000 people visited his coffin, in Menlo Park, New Jersey when he died. People across the nation turned off their "lights" at 10:00 pm the night of his funeral to pay respect to the one people called the Father of the Modern World. He was the Wizard of Menlo Park. So, what set him apart?

The obvious qualities of Mr. Edison are:

- He was curious and always on the hunt to improve everyday life.
- He was willing to learn about unfamiliar and uncomfortable arenas.
- He was a problem-solver who wanted to fix things people needed fixing.
- He didn't let failure stop him from tenaciously finding creative solutions.
- He was ambitious, working well into the night for breakthroughs.

Thomas Edison once said his greatest blessing was his lack of formal education. While informal experimentation took longer, he felt teachers might try to convince him that what he planned was impossible. After failing in the classroom, Tom was encouraged to leave the school system as a young boy. He later admitted, "I was always at the foot of the class. I used to feel the teachers did not sympathize with me and my father thought I was stupid." He decided what he lacked in education, he'd make up for in ambition. By then, he believed people don't learn nearly as much in a "classroom" as in a "lab." So, into a lab he ventured, as a young man. But it wasn't easy or fast for Tom Edison. Check out these little known facts about him...

1. He was removed from formal school and considered a failure.

2. He was withdrawn, shy and found social situations difficult.

3. He was partially deaf for most of his life, beginning at 12 years old.

4. His experiments ended up burning down barns and other buildings.

5. He was a poor businessman losing millions of dollars over his lifetime.

So what did he have going for him? He was an eternal optimist and incurably tenacious. Although he was often ridiculed, Thomas Edison made over ten thousand attempts before finally demonstrating the world's first working light bulb in 1879. Asked by a reporter how it felt to fail ten thousand times, Edison replied frankly: "I did not fail ten thousand times. The light bulb was an invention with ten thousand steps."

Like many others we remember as brilliant, Edison made progress through extensive trial and error, believing he did not fail thousands of times—he simply found thousands of ways his idea would not work. It was all seen as progress. You may remember his most famous statement: "Success is one percent inspiration and ninety nine percent perspiration."

What's the Big Deal About 212 Degrees?

Mr. Edison is a brilliant example of this *Habitude*. Let me explain. At 211 degrees, water is very hot. At 212 degrees, it boils. And with boiling comes steam. It can power a train or a steamboat, moving tons of weight to a destination.

Just one degree different and everything changes. When the heat is turned up just a notch, the outcome of the game can change. It's that little extra. Hall of Fame NFL coach Vince Lombardi said it this way: "Inches make a champion."

It's true. The last time I looked, the average difference between first and second place in one year's PGA championships was 1.71 strokes. That's less than a half stroke a day. The difference in what they took home? First place winners received $460,657 more. The difference between first and second place in a recent NASCAR Daytona 500 race was 0.175 seconds. In the Olympics, we always see the power of 212 degrees. The margin of victory in the Men's Giant Slalom was 0.17 seconds. In the Men's 800-meter race, it was 0.21 seconds. In Women's 1,000-meter speed skating, it was 0.07 seconds. The difference between first and second is not talent at this level. It's the heat.

The Difference Drive Makes

Tom Edison simply turned up the heat one degree, and turned out a thousand patents over his career. It was that little extra he gave—the attitude, the effort, the curiosity, the passion—that set him apart. He was consumed with improving people's lives. And this reality sets nearly all achievers apart from the rest.

According to one study done on a hundred high achievers in music, sales, business, athletics and art, researchers sought to identify the greatest commonalities those achievers shared. Their hypothesis, predictably, was that it would be giftedness or early advantages that gave them a head start.

The fact is, they were surprised with their findings. The single greatest factor for success was not giftedness or social status. It was *drive*. They found that each person lived at 212 degrees.[3]

How Hungry are You?

What motivates a man or woman plays a huge role in whether they get what they're after or not. In fact, I've found each of us should answer three big questions:

1. **What do you really want in life? (This is about your desire)**

2. **Why do you want it? (This is about your motives)**

3. **How badly do you want it? (This is about your passion)**

What's your answer to these? It has been said that one's destiny is not determined by what he possesses, but by what possesses him. Passion is a vital ingredient in a fulfilling life. It's the energy of the soul. It's often the difference between good and great, more so than IQ, talent, assets or networking skills. Passion is that internal fire that gives an intangible advantage to those who have it.

It is probably no coincidence that over 50 percent of Fortune 500 CEO's had a C to C- grade point average in school. More than 50 percent of self-made millionaires never finished college, and 75 percent of U.S. presidents were in the lower half of their class academically. So how did they get reach such peaks? For most—it was passion and grit. They were hungry. That's what frequently moves a person from mediocrity to excellence. It's more about attitude than aptitude. It's the one-degree extra.

So Why Do so Many Lack the Extra Degree?

Do you know anyone who's passionate? Someone you'd say that "passion" describes her life? Why do you think passion is so rare? Why do people lack it? Why do so few people live at 212 degrees? Let me suggest a few reasons to talk over:

1. They've allowed something precious to become common or routine.

2. They've become distracted by multitudes of voices that cry for their attention.

3. They don't believe their involvement makes a real difference.

4. They fail to catch a vision for something beyond themselves.

5. They've seen no models of passion or excellence.

Unfortunately, this is the story of so many. We begin our careers well, but fade over time. Perhaps we get cynical, worn out, or we just get beat up by tough circumstances. But like a slow tire leak…many people run out of air. They hit "auto pilot." They lose all the steam in their engines. One study shows disengaged employees cost U.S. businesses $11 billion annually.[4]

So let me ask you a question. Don't you think Tom Edison had a right to "run out of steam" when he failed to produce a working light bulb after 9,000 attempts? Something kept him going. Sure he was intelligent, but so were many of his contemporaries who never accomplished anything but survival. In fact, many of them weren't shy, could hear fine, knew how to manage money and lived on the right side of the tracks, socially.

But they were content to exist at 211 degrees. They merely survived.

What if You Turned Up the Heat?

- What if you invested a few "extra degree" hours a month to your own personal development? That would equal weeks of growth this year.

- What if you eliminated 30 minutes of TV each day and spent that time with family? That equals over 182 extra hours each year.

- What if you gave a few extra hours a month to the mission of your business? That could be the equivalent of one extra full week a year.

I know people who have done these very things. They chose to invest their time differently, and see what a difference it made. None of them have switched back. Michelangelo once said, "The danger for most of us lies not in setting our aim too high and falling short, but in setting our aim too low and achieving our mark."

Joe Dimaggio is one of the greatest baseball players of all time. Joltin' Joe led the New York Yankees to nine World Series titles in 13 seasons. Late in his career, Joe continued to play with passion, long after he was assured of making it into the Hall of Fame. After one game, a reporter asked Dimaggio why he still played with such gusto. After all, he didn't need to prove himself anymore. I love Joe's response. He explained there were two reasons he played so hard. First, he said, he still got excited every time he put on that Yankee uniform. Second, he knew there was always one person in the stands who'd never seen Joe Dimaggio play. Hence, Joe kept the heat at 212 degrees.

Maybe it's time we turned the heat up too.

Reflect and Respond

1. Talk over why passion is so rare in people? (Start with the list above)

_____

_____

2. Can you provide an example of when you displayed passion for a project?

_____

_____

3. Joe Dimaggio played passionately because he loved his organization and wanted to model passion. What are your best reasons for working with passion?

_____

_____

SELF ASSESSMENT

Consider two common tasks you perform at work, one that energizes you, and the other you just endure. Jot them down below and evaluate your level of passion:

1. A Task That Energizes You:

_____

Why such passion?
- I see how the task fits our mission
- I love this task; it fits my gifts
- It see how it helps others out
- Other:_____

2. A Task You Feel No Passion For:

_____

Why no passion?
- I see little point in the task
- It requires no real talent
- I'm not cut out to do the task
- Other:_____

EXERCISE

Choose one repeated project you perform on your job. It might even make for a good experiment to select one you don't feel especially passionate about. In other words, you don't execute it at 212 degrees.

For an entire week, turn the heat up as you pursue this task. Locate ways you could "go the extra mile" and perform beyond what is expected. Do more than the job description requires you to do. For discussion afterward, write down the ways you demonstrated passion for the task. Then, ask yourself: Did working with passion actually end up providing a little more passion? In other words, did acting passionate eventually give you passion inside? Did the emotion follow the action? Talk about it.

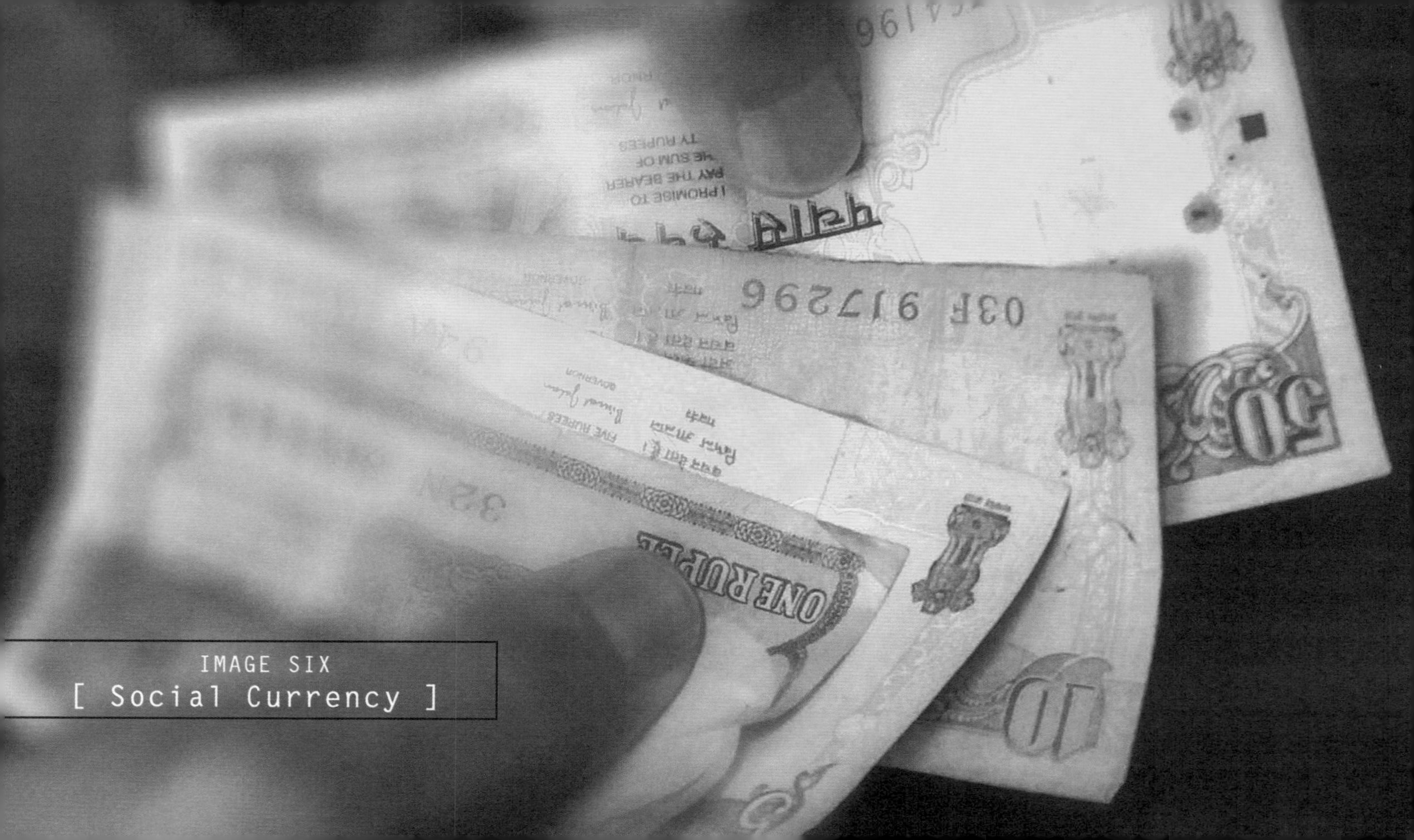

IMAGE SIX

[Social Currency]

Social Currency

PUBLIC SUPPORT EARNS A TEAM MEMBER PRIVATE INFLUENCE WITH THEIR
SUPERVISOR. IT'S THE MOST VALUABLE CURRENCY TO SENIOR LEADERS.

I've had the privilege of traveling to over fifty countries around the world on almost
every continent. Our organization, Growing Leaders, has developed partnerships
in dozens of nations, and I've loved visiting various cultures through my career.

You can imagine, I have a drawer full of money—loose change and bills—from
each of these countries that I've accumulated over time. Money looks different in
each country, with various colors of ink, icons, denominations and symbols. But
one thing is for sure. Each bill has a value in the country where it belongs. But
often…only there.

I learned a valuable lesson the hard way years ago.

I was in Singapore and had brought some cash with me from my last trip to Asia.
I felt good about being able to use my leftover money from a previous exchange
there. When making a purchase at a shopping mall, however, I got a shock. I
handed the store clerk some money—and got a strange look from her. When I
asked what was wrong, she smiled and said, "Sir, this money isn't good here. It
looks like it's from the Philippines."

I looked at it closely and suddenly grew embarrassed. Sure enough, she was right.
I was trying to buy something in a foreign country with the wrong cash.

As ridiculous as this story sounds, it is a picture of a principle every team member
needs to learn at work. Each company and each supervisor has a certain currency
you can spend at work. It's not financial. It's social currency. It's learning to interact
with bosses and colleagues in a way that both parties can *give* and *receive* what's
needed. It works like cash—but it's actually more valuable. When the proper social
currency is used, everyone wins. Both relationships and results improve.

Michael Jordan continues to be one of the most recognized names in the world. He led the Chicago Bulls to six NBA championships in eight years from 1991-1998. He remains one of the greatest basketball players in the history of the game.

It was during his playing days that Michael learned this principle. The Bulls didn't win a championship for several years with Jordon on the team. It wasn't until Phil Jackson took over as head coach that the Bulls figured out how to win it all. I believe it was a combination of talent, leadership and MJ modeling this *Habitude*: Social Currency.

How did Jordan build social currency on the team?

1. **He led himself well**
   MJ often stayed after practice an extra thirty minutes, shooting free throws. His teammates respected him as he practiced hard and played hard. He became a leader because he didn't ask anyone to do what he wouldn't do himself.

2. **He lightened the load of his coach**
   MJ and Phil Jackson formed a great relationship. He listened to his coach, and became an extension of him, by providing direction to the team, both on and off the court. Aligned with the style of his head coach, MJ helped shape the team.

3. **He was willing to do what others wouldn't do**
   MJ stretched everyone on the team by setting standards and living by them in his job as a guard or short forward. He did what most players refused to do in his work ethic. He modeled the way in scoring, rebounds, defense, assists, etc.

4. **He cultivated honest relationships with teammates**
   As the Bulls groomed the talents of Horace Grant, Scottie Pippen and Dennis Rodman, Michael earned the right to get in their faces if he felt they weren't performing at their potential. He had hard conversations to pull out their best.

5. **He publicly supported his coach, teammates and organization**
   Finally, although MJ was a competitor, he accumulated social currency by always supporting his coach and teammates in public statements. He backed the Bulls organization in public, which earned him influence with them in private.

This is how team members in any industry gain social currency. When you perform well and represent the organization well in public, you receive great credibility to influence that organization behind closed doors. My friend, author Andy Stanley, says it this way: *Loyalty publicly results in leverage privately.*

Think about it. Michael Jordan wasn't the head coach, but he certainly led the team. It was not about a position but a disposition...earned through social currency.

I learned this principle in my twenties, under John Maxwell. He had a rule: Our team would practice public solidarity. If anyone approached one of us with a gripe or some gossip about another team member, we would do our best to solve the problem, but we'd back up our team member publicly. We stood together. In private, we had some very candid conversations between us, as teammates, to find if there was any truth to a complaint, but we always supported each other publicly. It felt a little like a family. We never let an outsider (customer) break us up or come between us. We worked to get results, and do it with integrity as a team.

It was liberating to know it was all for one and one for all. It fostered mutual respect for our leader and teammates. It enabled us to brainstorm solutions to problems, argue with each other in private, yet encourage each other in our various departments. And all of us could then support our leader. What you do in private impacts what you do in public and vice versa. Former Army General and Secretary of State Colin Powell once said, "When we are debating an issue, loyalty means giving me your honest opinion, whether you think I'll like it or not. Disagreement, at this stage, stimulates me. But once a decision has been made, the debate ends. From that point on, loyalty means executing the decision as if it were your own."

Leading Up

Dee Hock, founder of Visa International, calls this principle "leading up." When we talk about leadership we usually mean leading those who are under our care. You'll have opportunities, however, to "lead up" and influence those who are over you—your boss, supervisor, or manager. Again, it's not by a position but a disposition. There are certain behaviors we can practice that earn the right to influence those in authority. In fact, practicing this *Habitude* actually allows you to "lead up"…not kiss up.

If you want to influence your boss…

Back in 1995, I wrote a book on mentoring. It's been updated and now is called, *lifeGIVING Mentors*. In it, I talk about influencing people from anywhere in an organization. I use the word INFLUENCE as a reminder of how we earn the right to sway others:

I – INVEST IN PEOPLE. Prepare, and make deposits in their life and interests.

N – NATURAL WITH PEOPLE. Be authentic and sincere. People can smell a fake.

F – FAITH IN PEOPLE. Demonstrate that you believe in them and in their work.

L – LISTENING TO PEOPLE. You gain respect and a voice by showing it to others.

U – UNDERSTANDING OF PEOPLE. Make an effort to know what makes them tick.

E – ENCOURAGEMENT TO PEOPLE. This is the oxygen of the soul. We all need it.

N – NAVIGATE FOR PEOPLE. Don't be afraid to offer ideas that add value.

C – COMPASSION FOR PEOPLE. Genuine influence comes from care and concern.

E – ENTHUSIASM OVER PEOPLE. Passion for the cause and for others is magnetic.

Social currency begins accumulating with your first encounters. Look your boss in the eye when interacting. Be a few minutes early and put your phone aside when meeting. Be professional yet warm with them, and mirror their tone in conversation. Develop emotional intelligence (EQ), which enables you to know when to display emotion and when to delay emotion. Both are necessary. And always remember—question decisions in private, and support decisions in public.

Who's Got the Gun?

Let me close with a picture. In their book, *Managing Up*, Michael and Deborah Dobson suggest a fitting analogy for social currency. Imagine you're in doctor's office. Patients are in the waiting room and all is calm, when a person walks in with a gun. Everyone can see it. Instantly that person has influence. They have the power to control people's behavior. We commonly assume that to persuade them, we'd have to get a gun ourselves. No doubt, that would be the easiest way to do it.

But, we've all heard stories of someone who talked someone out of shooting a gun, or committing a crime, or even committing suicide. It was done through trust and relationship. To influence in that context—you must earn it.

The same is true with positions in an organization. At the risk of sounding crass: your boss has the gun. Their position lends them the power to change behavior. Brilliant leaders don't lean on their position (their gun) but develop trusting relationships among team members. Those on the team don't have the advantage of having any gun. They MUST cultivate their influence in other ways. I believe it's done best through discovering what the *social currency* is in your workplace and leveraging it effectively. When I began working with John Maxwell at twenty-three years old, I learned quickly that his most valuable currency was "*time.*" When I saved him time by helping him on a project, I gained all kinds of influence. A colleague of mine had a boss whose currency was "*accuracy.*" Another friend told me her supervisor's currency was "*loyalty.*" Once you understand this principle—you can earn dividends regardless of your title.

Reflect and Respond

1. Practicing this *Habitude* can be easily seen as "kissing up" or "sucking up" to the boss. Why are we so suspicious of people who publicly support a boss?

_____

_____

2. Have you seen a team member build social currency with their boss and gain influence in the process? What have you observed?

_____

_____

3. It's been said, "Gossip is poor communication's offspring." What's this mean?

_____

_____

4. What could you do today to build trust and gain influence at work?

_____

_____

SELF ASSESSMENT

Reflect on a relatively controversial decision that has surfaced at work; one in which people disagree and tend to talk about in private conversations. How do you respond? Place a number (1 through 5) indicating what you're most prone to do:

- Remain silent and just listen to others   _____

- Speak up and support your boss' decision   _____

- Initiate a conversation with colleagues to talk about it   _____

- Join in the gossip and ponder out loud why they did it   _____

- Set up a meeting to ask your boss about the decision   _____

Discuss your tendencies. Do you naturally earn social currency with your supervisor?

EXERCISE

This week, watch for opportunities to genuinely foster trust and collaboration among team members by speaking well of your organization's mission, your supervisor, and his/her current decisions. Evaluate how it feels: Do you feel like a fake? Does it feel natural or unnatural? Is it seen by team members as artificial or genuine?

If the opportunity arises, schedule a brief time to talk with your supervisor about a decision you don't understand. Express that you're seeking to understand so you can support the move and align your actions with it. Was any trust built?

Evaluate and discuss how social currency works in your workplace afterward.

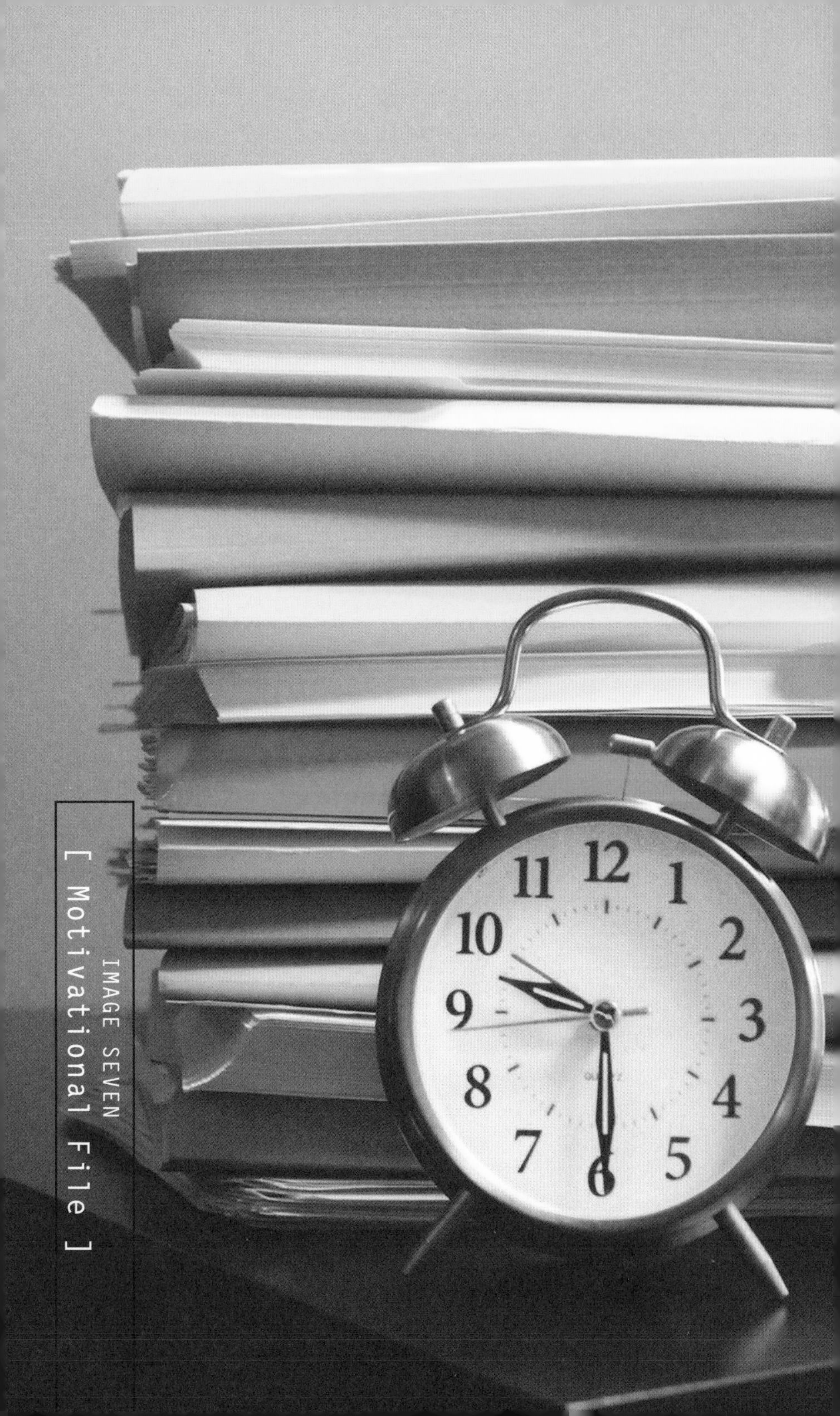

IMAGE SEVEN

[Motivational File]

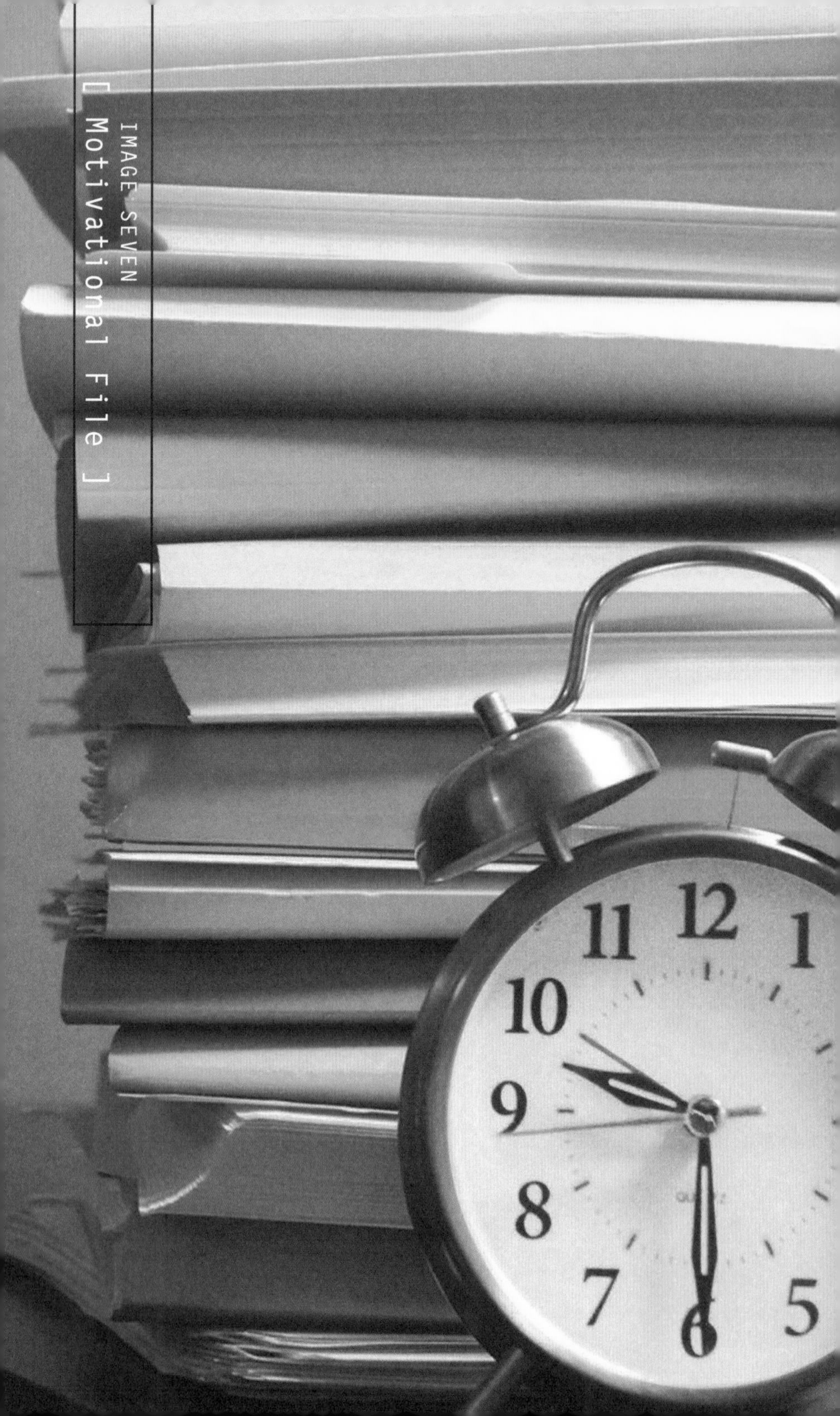

IMAGE SEVEN

[Motivational File]

Motivational File

CREATIVE PEOPLE TEND TO BE CRITICAL BECAUSE THEY SEE POSSIBILITIES OTHERS DON'T. INSTEAD OF COMPLAINING, START A FILE FULL OF IDEAS BEGINNING WITH: I WOULD...

William McKnight was a giant in the business world, serving as chairman of the board for the innovative 3M Company between 1949-1966. McKnight would often spot an employee working on a new invention and ask about it. The employee would light up and excitedly explain the cool new product he was creating. McKnight realized this kind of energy and creativity was the future of 3M. From time to time, he'd encourage employees to finish their assigned tasks as quickly as they could, so they could work on their "invention." At times, he'd keep the lights on after hours so team members could keep creating. It was this extra time that enabled the "birth" of several new products:

- Wet-or-dry waterproof sandpaper

- Scotch masking tape

- Scotch transparent tape

- Colorquartz roofing granules

- Rubber cement

3M even developed a philosophy to foster creativity. They gave every employee 15 percent of their workweek just to try out new ideas of their choosing. This led to dozens of inventions you and I use today. For instance, 3M scientist Art Fry and his team mates used their "15 percent" to create the perfect bookmark for his church hymnal: Post-it Notes. Today, most every office in America uses Post-it Note pads.

McKnight's basic rule of management was laid out in 1948:

> *As our business grows, it becomes increasingly necessary to delegate responsibility and to encourage men and women to exercise their initiative. This requires considerable tolerance. Those men and women, to whom we delegate authority and responsibility, if they are good people, are going to want to do their jobs in their own way. Mistakes will be made. But if a person is essentially right, the mistakes he or she makes are not as serious in the long run as the mistakes management will make if it undertakes to tell those in authority exactly how they must do their jobs. Management that is destructively critical when mistakes are made kills initiative. And it's essential that we have many people with initiative if we are to continue to grow.*

What's a Motivation File?

Whether or not you work for an organization that celebrates this kind of creativity, you can practice a simple principle that fosters personal creativity and prevents you from becoming negative when your ideas get turned down. I call it a: "Motivation File." This little idea is one I have practiced for almost three decades now thanks to a mentor of mine, Keith Drury.

The idea is built off of three basic notions:

1. Creative people can tend to be critical
   Why? Because they can see what others cannot see. They seem to be able to envision how to make things better; how to improve products, events, music, ideas and art. Because they are so imaginative, they don't know why others don't find ways to improve their current "mediocre" work.

2. Criticism is de-motivating
   I probably don't need to convince you of this one. When you or someone else becomes critical, the atmosphere can get negative. The more the criticism, the greater the chances of things turning sour and becoming de-motivating. This can have an adverse affect on anyone.

3. The more creative you are, the greater your risk of de-motivation
   Therefore, if the first two notions above are accurate, then creative people are vulnerable to being a bit disheartened and unmotivated. If A = B, and B = C, then A = C. Let's face it. There's nothing more common than creative people who sit around and do nothing with their talent. Ideas don't become realities.

To combat this, we need to start a "Motivation File." This means, the moment you see something that could be better, instead of saying: "These people don't get it. I don't know why they do things that way. They should…"

Stop.

Instead, grab something to write on and begin with the statement: "In this situation, I would…" Never again criticize others for not doing something right or improving current realities. Turn it into a positive. Jot notes to yourself about what YOU would do if you were in charge. Then, throw that idea into a file. Perhaps it could even remain on your smart phone. Wherever you put it, the mere act of writing it down and filing it away can channel your emotional energy from negative and critical to positive and creative. Then, when you do get an opportunity, you have a "garden" of ideas to pull from. It's a motivation file.

It Really Works

For years, when I served in an associate role or a vice president role, I practiced this principle. I kept a drawer full of ideas in a folder, and years later implemented once I left my position in San Diego and had larger responsibilities in Denver and Atlanta back in the 1990s. Keeping this file enabled me to remain positive and engaged at my current positions, but always looking forward to opportunities where I could implement my own ideas. Once in a while, I even took the ideas to my supervisor—and inquired about implementing them right then and there. Once in a while, we did.

My point is, however, that simply keeping the file kept me positive and engaged. I avoided turning into a complainer who became disengaged. I kept my creative juices flowing. Today, as president of *Growing Leaders*, I've launched an "Idea Farm" where every team member can submit written ideas in a specific spot whenever they come to mind. (It's like a corporate Motivation File). We review new ideas on a regular basis as an entire team. We call it a "farm" because each idea is planted like a seed, knowing that some will actually come to fruition. I have found this accomplishes two goals:

1. THE IDEA FARM KEEPS IDEAS CONSTANTLY FLOWING, SEVERAL OF WHICH WE ARE ABLE TO IMPLEMENT TO IMPROVE OUR TEAM'S PRODUCTIVITY.

2. THE IDEA FARM KEEPS PEOPLE IN A POSITIVE AND PRODUCTIVE MINDSET, EVEN WHEN IDEAS ARE NOT ADOPTED. EVERYONE GETS HEARD.

Years ago, Edwin Cox was a door-to-door salesman trying to sell cookware products to housewives. His sales were doing poorly; no one seemed interested in the latest cookware technology. He usually didn't even get to demonstrate what he was selling. When Ed asked around, he discovered his colleagues weren't selling much either. He decided the company needed to come up with a gift—something they could give to consumers for free.

Cox pondered what customers really needed, and remembered many complaining about how hard it was to wash pots and pans. He went home and dipped small, square steel wool pads into a soapy solution. He would dry the pads and then re-dip them over and over again until they were saturated with dry soap.

These pads got him in the door. So, Edwin Cox took the idea to his supervisors, suggesting the pads could increase sales. When he got a less than passionate response, he decided instead of arguing about it, he'd just use them himself. The pad became his "motivation file." His sales took off.

Within a matter of months, it became clear customers were more interested in the scouring pads than the cookware. Cox started his own business manufacturing these soap pads. I bet you've heard of them. His wife created the name of S.O.S. Pads, "Save Our Saucepans." Rather than complaining about his current hardship, Cox created something revolutionary for kitchen clean up.

What We Really Want

Over the last several decades, research has been done on what employees want most from their workplace. In one of the most elaborate studies on employee motivation, involving 44,000 men and women, the Minneapolis Gas Company sought to determine what their potential employees desire most from a job. This 20-year study was quite revealing. The top responses were:

- A secure place to work.
- A creative place to work.
- An opportunity to grow.
- A company they're proud to work for.

Surprisingly, factors such as pay, benefits and working conditions were given a low rating by both groups. Contrary to common belief, money is not the prime motivator.[5]

The fact is—ideas are much more powerful motivators than money. Steve Jobs and his friend Steve Wozniak launched a little company in 1976 to sell a homemade computer that Wozniak designed called the Apple I. At the time, Jobs was twenty-one years old. What you may not know is—these two young entrepreneurs offered their invention to executives at Hewlett Packard and Commodore. Both turned them down. They just didn't see a future in personal computers. Fortunately for us, Steve Jobs didn't give up on his "motivation file" and ventured out to launch a company. The original Apple logo was a picture of Isaac Newton under an apple tree, with the inscription, "Newton…A Mind Forever Voyaging Through Strange Seas of Thought…Alone."

How about starting your own "Motivation File" this week and see if it just might be inspiring for you, and help you keep those creative juices flowing.

Reflect and Respond

1. Talk about a time you came up with a creative idea. Did you kill it...or execute the idea? Did you become unmotivated when others didn't get it?

_____

_____

2. What are the potential pitfalls of keeping a motivation file?

_____

_____

3. What are the potential advantages of keeping one at your workplace?

_____

_____

Self Assessment

Consider your own personal style. Circle the number which best describes what you do when others don't embrace ideas. When you get an idea, do you normally respond:

| I keep it inside | 1 2 3 4 5 6 7 8 9 10 | I share with others |

| I let it go and forget about it | 1 2 3 4 5 6 7 8 9 10 | I get frustrated at others' apathy |

| I decide it's not likely to change | 1 2 3 4 5 6 7 8 9 10 | I write it down and save it |

Discuss your tendency: do you neglect the idea or somehow keep it alive?

Exercise

This week, if you haven't done so already, start your own "motivation file." Keep a folder (either hard copy or digital) of ideas you've considered and write them down. In fact, in the space below, jot down two or three immediate ideas that come to mind, which you could either use later at the appropriate time or bounce off your supervisor.

If Steve Jobs was right—"Innovation distinguishes between a leader and follower"—Which one are you?

IMAGE EIGHT

[Microscopes and Telescopes]

Microscopes and Telescopes

ONE IS ABOUT DETAILS; THE OTHER ABOUT DISTANCE. WHEN EVALUATING
YOURSELF USE THE MICROSCOPE; WHEN EVALUATING OTHERS USE THE TELESCOPE.

For several years, NASA scientists have been working on the James Webb Space
Telescope, the most powerful telescope ever created. The telescope is said to be
capable of capturing seven times more light than the Hubble Space Telescope, a
factor that will aid in our exploration of the deepest reaches of outer space. The
$8.8 billion telescope will be massive, with its largest mirror, a unique folding,
18-segmented creation, spanning over 21 feet in length and weighing in excess
of 1500 pounds. Believe it or not, the mirror is six times larger than that of the
Hubble Telescope. These kinds of instruments will not only allow us to see out into
a distance, but across time. NASA reports it will allow astronomers to see 200 years
beyond the origin of the solar system.[6] It's absolutely incredible.

I've always marveled at telescopes. When I've looked through smaller ones, I am
amazed at how those stars, planets or satellites I observed with the naked eye became
so much larger and clearer with the simple use of a lens.

In contrast, microscopes do just the opposite. The world's most powerful
microscope, which resides in a specially constructed room at the University of
Victoria, has now been fully assembled and tested, and has a lineup of scientists
and businesses eager to use it. The seven ton, 4.5-metre tall Scanning Transmission
Electron Holography Microscope (STEHM), is the first such microscope of its
type in the world. With assembly complete, Dr. Rodney Herring and his team from
Hitachi were able to finally test the microscope. The results are the start of a new era
in scientific research. Dr. Herring said, "This enables us to see the unseen world."

We can now view gold atoms through the microscope at a resolution of 35
picometres. One picometre is a trillionth of a metre. This resolution is much better
than the previous best image with 49-picometre resolution taken at the Lawrence
Berkley National Laboratory in California, and is about 20 million times human
sight. This new microscope allows researchers to see atoms in a manner never before
possible. It certainly enables us to see objects in far more detail than the microscopes
we used in our college science class.

What These Instruments Teach Us

Here's my point in telling you about the telescope and the microscope.

Both of these instruments provide context, enabling us to see things more clearly. Centuries ago, people believed the earth was at the center of the universe, and the sun revolved around the earth, hence giving us sunrises and sunsets. Even though we still use those terms, we now understand it's the earth that revolves around the sun. We are not the center of our solar system. And peering through a *telescope*, men like Galileo saw the truth about the Copernican theory and explained it to a skeptical world.

Similarly, Joseph Lister had a difficult time convincing doctors to wash their hands before performing surgery on patients back in the 19th century. It required many deaths on the operating table to get them to listen. Then, he finally demonstrated through a *microscope* how germs contaminated our bodies. Thanks to his theory on germs—and our ability to see their details—he saved the lives of millions of people who prior to that, died from infection on the operating table.

Context Always Explains Conduct

And so it is with people. They can be funny. They can be irritating. They can seem to act strangely. You will find all kinds of people in your workplace, acting out in all kinds of ways, behaving differently than you. You'll be tempted to instantly judge them, and form an incomplete opinion. You may need to peer through an imaginary "telescope" to see the big picture and gain an explanation to their behavior. Once you look further and discover the context of their life, it likely will clarify their conduct.

Case in point. A man sat in a restaurant, staring at the ceiling, while his three young sons wreaked havoc over their booth and the rest of the café. The boys were screaming, running around, bumping into other tables—but the father just sat there, doing nothing. The other customers couldn't figure out why he wasn't a more attentive dad, quieting those boys down. He surely wasn't a very good disciplinarian to his kids, they assumed. When a customer finally demanded that a waitress talk to the man, she agreed, but offered a quick explanation. "I discovered a moment ago," she said, "that man just buried his wife—the mother of those three young kids. They've just returned from the funeral. I think they're still figuring out how to cope with their loss."

Context always explains conduct. Those simple facts enabled the other customers to be a little more empathetic toward the man. They simply needed a bigger perspective. They needed to look through a telescope to see past the immediate circumstances.

So here's my question for you. Who in your workplace might be facing difficult or even stressful personal situations, and perhaps their actions at work need patience from you, not judgment? Is it possible to look past their flaws and see their needs?

I have noticed something about myself. It is easy for me to judge myself with my "heart" but judge others with my "head" when I really need to do the opposite. In other words, when I do something wrong—I know exactly why it happened. I find myself excusing my poor performance by saying to myself: *I had such a hard day. Its no wonder I failed to follow through.* (I call that judging with the heart). However, when others fail, I can be quick to level a harsh judgment on them, believing they should have performed better or at least communicated about their inability to perform. (I call that judging with the head). In reality, I find life goes better when I reverse the two: I need to evaluate myself with mental toughness and evaluate others with empathy.

In short, I need to pull out the *microscope* when measuring myself, looking at every detail in order to continually improve. Then, I need to pull out the *telescope* when measuring others, recognizing there is likely a great reason for their conduct. I often must see at a distance to gain the context of their behavior.

I remember attending a business conference years ago. I was convinced to go because the keynote speaker was supposed to be an incredible communicator—very funny and very motivational. My colleagues persuaded me it would be worth the time. When the man got up to speak, he was anything but inspiring. In fact, he seemed a little flat. No humor. No inspiration. Just facts and case studies. I was unimpressed.

At dinner that night, someone stopped by our table and asked about the conference. I spoke up frankly and said I thought the speaker wasn't that good at all. It was at that point I heard the reason why. That speaker had just been told by a doctor that his son was dying. Their only chance of prolonging his life would be treatment in another state, requiring their family to move. He would lose his job. Not a good week.

The truth is—that speaker had every right to be sober and serious in his speech. When I heard the news about his son, I marveled that he was even able to do the speech. What a difference a little context makes. I also got a gut check on my predisposition to judge people so quickly. I decided to reserve my criticism of speakers until I got more facts. In summary, what I really needed after that conference was a telescope for seeing the big picture of that speaker's life and a microscope to see my own flaws.

KEEPING THE BIG PICTURE IN MIND...

In our office, we take steps to foster this *Habitude*. We stock our kitchen with food and allow our team members to eat for free—as long as they eat with someone else. They don't' have to talk about work, but we want to cultivate "community" among our people. We've found when we lubricate relationships the team just runs smoother.

In addition, we host a weekly Lunch and Learn on Mondays. During this time, our entire team eats together and we share what's happening in both our personal lives and our professional lives. Then, we spend time on personal growth, discussing a significant leadership principle and applying it to our lives.

We also hold a weekly "Stand Up" meeting, where we stand in a circle, and preview the major priorities each of team member that week. We write them down on a large white wall. We remain standing to keep the meeting short and sweet. It keeps us accountable and supportive of each other. It also insures communication and understanding.

Research shows that "when judging others, we tend to over-attribute acts to people's personalities rather than to the variables in a specific situation. This is why therapists separate problematic acts from the person. In short, it enables them to judge the *sin*, not the *sinner*. Our commitments to our judgments ought to be based on the depth of our knowledge. It's probably also true that pessimistic judgments about others are more likely to be damaging or injurious."[8]

So here's the rule I follow: *The further out I can see, the better the decision or judgment I make today.* In other words, when I gain the facts and see the reality associated with the circumstance, I tend to think more objectively. Further, when I see the impact of my judgment on the future of my relationships or the organization, I judge more wisely. One of the most quoted phrases Jesus of Nazareth spoke 2,000 years ago centered on this subject. He said, *"First take the log out of your own eye, then you can see to take the speck out of your brother's eye."* If I'm going to do this well, I've got to have a *telescope* and a *microscope*. Marianne Williamson wrote, "It takes courage… to endure the sharp pains of self discovery rather than choose to take the dull pain of unconsciousness that would last the rest of our lives."

Not far from where I was born, there is an old covered bridge. The road is narrow on that bridge, so the city council decided to put a "Yield" sign at the entrance of both sides. Cars coming in either direction know to look and yield to the oncoming traffic. What a great way to approach relationships at work. What if everyone was practicing this *Habitude*, insuring relationships are good because we all look out for each other. Sounds to me like a great place to work.

Reflect and Respond

1. We live in a disposable society. How does this make us less willing to work at relationships?

_____

_____

2. Have you ever seen poor perspective make people jump to wrong conclusions?

_____

_____

3. Have you seen "context" explain conduct? How so?

_____

_____

Self Assessment

Consider your own personal perspective. Circle the number that best describes what you do when things go wrong:

I look outward at other's flaws	1 2 3 4 5	I look inward at my flaws
I jump to conclusions quickly	1 2 3 4 5	I wait and gather all the facts
I assume the worst about others	1 2 3 4 5	I believe the best about others
I focus on critiquing others	1 2 3 4 5	I focus on critiquing myself

Discuss your tendency: Are you easier on yourself or on others when you evaluate?

_____

_____

_____

Exercise

This week, stay alert for an opportunity to practice this *Habitude*. When something goes wrong, pause and reflect. What's your natural inclination? Instead of assuming someone else is fully to blame, look for changes you could make to improve the outcome. What happens to your attitude when you immediately pick up a *microscope*? What happens when you peer through a *telescope* to see the big picture before assuming the worst about others?

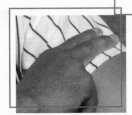

The Steal Sign

EARL WEAVER'S RULE WAS: DON'T STEAL A BASE WITHOUT MY SIGNAL. REGGIE JACKSON DID AND RUINED A GAME. LEADERS SEE WHAT OTHERS DON'T. TRUST IS A MUST.

In his book, *How Life Imitates the World Series*, Dave Boswell tells a story about how Earl Weaver, former manager of the Baltimore Orioles, handled his star, Reggie Jackson, back in 1976.

Weaver had a rule that a player could not steal a base unless given a steal sign. This upset Jackson because he felt he knew pitchers and catchers well enough to know whether he could steal off of them. In one game, Jackson was on first base and was not getting the signal to steal second. His manager obviously didn't know how smart or how fast he was. Jackson decided to steal without the signal from Weaver. He got a good lead, a great jump off the pitcher, and easily slid in safe at second base. Jackson smiled with delight, feeling he'd justified his judgment to his manager.

Later, Weaver pulled Jackson aside and explained why he hadn't given the steal sign. It wasn't because he didn't know how fast or how savvy Jackson was. The reason was much bigger than that. First, the next batter was Lee May, his best power hitter other than Jackson. When Jackson stole second, first base was left open, allowing the other team to walk May intentionally taking the bat right out of his hands. Second, the following hitter hadn't been strong against that pitcher, so Weaver felt he had to send up a pinch hitter to try to drive in the men on base. That left Weaver without bench strength later in the game when he needed it.

The problem was—Jackson saw only his relationship to the pitcher and catcher. Weaver saw the big picture of the entire game. It was quite a lesson for the superstar from his manager.

The story also illustrates a principle every new professional needs to learn. While no manager or supervisor is perfect, they are the most likely ones to understand the big picture of what's happening at work. They know the budget, the personnel, the deadlines, the history, the profit margins of the products or services—you get the idea. They don't know details of everything going on in the office, but they have holistic perspective. There will be times it will be difficult for you to understand certain moves, layoffs, promotions, or other decisions your leaders make. Especially when you don't have all the information, you may completely disagree with their judgment. Young team members usually have to learn to trust their managers through an experience like Reggie Jackson had with his manager. Very often bosses can't explain every detail as to why they made a decision—but team members usually do well to recognize they've given thought to that choice. Trust is earned and learned.

TRUST IS A MUST

I will never forget working under John Maxwell back in the early 1980s. John had just let Derin, (fictitious name) a well-liked manager, go. Needless to say, this decision was unpopular with those who worked on his team. Derin had a great personality and seemed to be getting his work done. Yet, John terminated him.

Maxwell began to get hateful letters and complaints—accusing him of cruelty and not understanding what was really going on. Several people met with him, asking him why he had fired Derin and even circulated a petition to re-hire him. Some people quit, when John didn't budge on his decision, nor explain why he'd made it.

As a young team member, I met with John and privately asked why he'd done it. Very discretely, John explained that Derin had embezzled money from the organization, lied about it and that, although he was married, he'd had an affair with another woman in the organization. John didn't want to make all this public as he was trying to help Derin salvage both his marriage and his reputation.

I watched John take the heat from all sides, but never once retaliate. It would have been easy for him to hang out Derin's "dirty laundry" and reveal how he'd cheated on both the organization and his wife. But in the interest of helping Derin and not smearing his name, John stood by his right decision and took friendly fire. He told me later he knew how life had a way of vindicating a leader's wise choices. Derin would either get his act together (and see a counselor), or we'd all see the error of his ways.

He was right. Within a year, the truth came out. Derin's misconduct became apparent and his marriage broke up. While it was sad to those of us who knew him, everyone else saw how John Maxwell had taken the high road in his leadership. It was through this experience, everyone learned to trust their leader.

- Both leadership and relationships operate on the basis of trust.

- When trust is diminished, so is energy, collaboration and creativity.

- At times team members must trust when they don't fully understand leaders.

- Trust works like an ocean tide. When it rises, all the boats (people) rise with it.

The problem is—trust is one of the most difficult elements to build into a workplace.

According to the American Psychological Association's 2014 Work and Well Being Survey, "...nearly 1 in 4 workers say they don't trust their employer and only about half believe their employer is open and upfront with them."[10] Usually fear and suspicion accompany a culture of distrust. People begin to be skeptical and afraid of taking risks. They start withholding information, and refuse to take initiative or extend themselves to others. In short, they become passive. They shift into survival mode, becoming self-protective and holding their cards close to their vest. This is a problem.

According to author Stephen M.R. Covey, business always operates at "the speed of trust." It's the one thing that changes everything at work. People follow the leader as closely as they trust him or her. Their work ethic reflects how much they feel trusted. Trust is not a luxury. It's a necessity.[11]

Let me give you a vivid analogy. Imagine for a moment, you're a soldier, and your troop is being fired upon by the enemy. You're all hiding in a bunker, but you know it's only a matter of time before you'll engage in hand to hand combat. Emotions are high. Stress is intense. What do you do? It's in these moments, soldiers are trained to trust their commanding officer. It's life and death—but no individual soldier can simply take matters into their own hands. You are a unit. You must work as a team—and the only way to do so, is to trust your leader. Lives are at stake.

Fortunately, the stakes are likely not this high for you today. Your issues probably surround sales, production, profit margins and customer satisfaction. But if you're going to operate effectively, you have the same need to work as a unit, trusting those who are in charge, even when you don't have all the facts. To be perfectly honest, that's when trust is most essential.

How difficult is it for you to trust others when you don't have all the facts?

WHAT HAPPENS IF YOU FEEL YOU CAN'T TRUST YOUR BOSS?

I often get the question—what if I can't trust my supervisor? What should I do? My answer is—it depends on why you feel you can't trust him or her. If it's due to incompetence, you must choose whether you can continue to grow in this workplace. If it's due to questionable ethics, you're dealing with another issue. Can you maintain yours even if colleagues fail to practice them? This will require careful reflection.

In general, if you're not sure you can trust your boss, I suggest you trust him anyway. I'm not endorsing naivety or passive allegiance, but acting out of hope for a change in behavior—you or him. Most human beings (bosses included), respond favorably to being trusted. If your trust is genuine and you listen respectfully to him, he's likely to reciprocate and trust you back. That's how trust works, and it is also how it spreads.

Trust requires respectful listening, which brings opportunities for self-improvement. Listening attentively with an open mind and heart can make a huge difference in one's ability to trust others. Trusting him or her may very well cultivate trustful behavior.

Trust is a two-way street. It cannot be imposed on someone, and it requires risk. The only way to find trust is to look for it and expect it in others. This is risky, yet it is the only way trust can build in any relationship. Keep in mind everyone wants to be trusted, and most people will make every effort to become trustworthy. In addition, most of us want feedback on how we're being perceived. As hard as it is for you to talk to your boss about untrustworthy behavior, if you're not alone in your mistrust, you may be surprised to find just how willing he is to listen and try to improve things.

The fact is, your career will work a little bit like a dance. You and your organization are moving back and forth, in sync with each other. At least you should be in sync. There is a give and a take. There should be no need to step on each other's toes as you dance. But you must follow the lead of your supervisor for things to flow. If you just can't do that, you may need to leave. Every team member should "get in or get out." Why? Because dancing with a partner involves choreography.

You can't just make it up and expect your partner to read your mind. There is a plan, and if the plan goes well, it appears as a beautiful, organic flow to all who watch.

The bottom line? If your manager says wait for the steal sign, I suggest you wait.

Reflect and Respond

1. Why is trust so powerful yet so difficult to experience with people?

_____

_____

2. Talk about past experiences you've had with trust and distrust. Is it hard for you to trust others? Has it been difficult for you to earn the trust of others?

_____

_____

3. Are there any current situations where you need to deepen your trust?

_____

_____

4. What is one step you could take to display trust in your leaders?

_____

_____

Self Assessment

Assess yourself below. How easy or difficult is it for you to trust teammates and leaders? Respond to the statement below rating your most honest answers. Put a "1" next to the most accurate answer, and follow suit all the way to "6."

When faced with a situation where you don't understand your leader's behavior...

_____ You tend to clam up, keep your head down and not ask any questions.

_____ You tend to talk to people, inquiring as to what they think about the situation.

_____ You tend to go directly to your supervisor and ask about the situation.

_____ You tend to go it alone and make up your mind as to how to respond.

_____ You tend to want to execute justice, suspecting trouble is on the way.

_____ You tend to flee, since authority figures haven't been trustworthy in your past.

Discuss your tendency: why do you respond the way you do?

Consider three situations where you find it challenging to trust someone at work. (It may be your direct supervisor or a fellow team member). Obviously, you can't force them to change—but you can choose to model trust, at least as long as it is warranted. Ask yourself—what would a trusting person do in this situation? If I choose to trust, how would I respond to the people in question? What is the proper behavior? Is the situation so confusing that you should go talk to your supervisor? Talk over your decisions to these situations.

Homes and Apartments

PEOPLE USUALLY TAKE BETTER CARE OF THEIR OWN HOME THAN THEY DO
AN APARTMENT BECAUSE IT BELONGS TO THEM. DON'T RENT YOUR WORK,
OWN IT.

I rented my first apartment between my sophomore and junior year of college. It
felt good to finally have my own place to live, outside of a college dorm. On moving
day, I realized that while the apartment building was new to me…it wasn't new at
all. The complex had been around for thirty years. While moving my furniture in,
I noticed the door had chipped paint, the side window was slightly cracked, the
front left burner in the kitchen didn't work and the carpet was badly worn in the
hallway. In fact, as each month passed, I made new discoveries of the imperfections
in my apartment.

All of this didn't matter a whole lot to me because it wasn't mine. I was only renting
the apartment for a year. In fact, I didn't take great care of the place during my stay
because I kept thinking: *I will only be here until next summer.*

My wife and I bought our first home in 1985. We'd been married for four years,
and had saved our money to purchase this new, start-up home in San Diego. We
had lived in apartments up till then—and I can't tell you how good it felt to actually
own something we could call ours. I will never forget doing the walk-through right
before we moved in. We carefully observed every nook and cranny of that place,
making sure the finishing touches were perfect. And over the next nine years that
we lived there, we were careful to take immaculate care of our home. After all, it
belonged to us.

OWNING VS. RENTING

I hope my point is clear and obvious. While I am not proud of myself for taking
better care of my purchased home than my rented apartment, the fact is, I did.
People in general tend to take better care of things they own than things they
rent temporarily.

When my son got his driver's license, he didn't have the money to buy a new car. So for a while, he drove his older sister's car. It got him from point A to point B, but I noticed he was nonchalant about its care. He later bought a car with his own money. It was a silver Jeep Cherokee, and it purred like a kitten. I was amazed at how motivated Jonathan became to do all needed repairs, to keep it clean and to insure it was ready for road trips. The difference between the two cars, of course, was the same as my apartment and my home. The moment he had to pay for the car—it was not loaned but earned—he was an owner who cared deeply about how it looked and performed. It was his baby.

Far too many new professionals enter their first jobs like they do an apartment. They aren't sure if this is a long-term thing, and they haven't really made up their minds about how long they want to stay in it. In fact, it may be they are still unsure about the direction of their career. Unfortunately, it's obvious to their employer—they are only half-hearted about their position. Their uncertainty causes them to "rent" their job instead of "owning" it. They don't take as good of care of it as they would if they really committed themselves and served as if it were their company. It shows up in little but real ways, such as:

- YOU'RE UNPREPARED FOR TEAM PROJECTS.

- YOU DON'T SHOW UP ON TIME FOR MEETINGS.

- YOU SEEM NONCHALANT ABOUT TASKS YOU WORK ON.

- YOU DON'T REALLY CARE ABOUT COLLEAGUES OUTSIDE THE JOB.

- YOU ARE CARELESS ABOUT YOUR WORKSPACE AND APPEARANCE.

- YOU DON'T REALLY PUSH YOURSELF TO WORK HARD AND BE CREATIVE.

The truth is—everyone is working for himself. You may think you aren't since you have a boss and are told what to do for the company. But in reality, you and your teammates are all working for themselves. The effort and energy you exert will either come back to haunt you or bless you in the end. Your work and attitude this week will eventually show up. Every day you are building your resume. My suggestion? Own it, don't rent it.

I'll be the first to admit, your career may look different than your parent's or grandparent's generation. In the past, people climbed a corporate ladder. They often stayed with a company for decades and step-by-step, climbed that ladder toward higher positions and better salaries. Many believe new professionals today have moved from "ladders" to "lily pads." Instead of climbing, it may look more like a frog hopping from one spot to another. You may even have multiple careers in various industries. You may not stay in one place for decades. Believe it or not—my advice is still the same. Own your career, don't rent it. Everywhere you find yourself, invest yourself wholly into the work. Give it everything you've got.

Ownership Brings Vision

When you own your career, you can better see and seize opportunities as they surface. Case in point: Levi Strauss. He arrived in San Francisco as a dreamer during the gold rush of the 1850s. He was a 17-year old immigrant tailor, who heard about the gold and wanted to cash in on the opportunity. He read of the overnight-fortunes made by those who discovered gold in California. But, alas he never found gold. He did find, however, a golden opportunity. Strauss quickly realized that many travelers arrived in great need of canvas for tents and covered wagons. He tailored large pieces of canvas and sold it to these miners, which made him enough money to stay. An astute observer of people's needs, he saw that these same miners were going through trousers fast, ripping them as they squatted, climbed, crawled and sat panning for gold. So he stitched the canvas into overalls and began selling them all over the place. They were stiff but sturdy and held up well. By the early 1860s, he traded in the canvas for denim. The cloth was originally from Genoa, and thus called Genes, and later spelled Jeans. Levi had himself a thriving business. Ironically, he made none of his money from the gold rush, at least directly. Levi Strauss never discovered gold…he did discover blue…as in blue jeans. And that made him richer than most gold diggers. The pants were stitched and held together with copper rivets because they were used as work clothes. Today, Levis are seldom worn as work clothes and mostly worn as a fashion statement. Designer jeans, the pants once designed for work, are now the costume of play and a multi-million dollar industry.

The Primary Motivator for Peak Performance

Something good happens when a people begin to "own" their work. Energy comes. They get creative, they get resourceful, and they take incredible pride in their work. Jon Katzenbach published research illustrating how team members who took pride in their work actually outperformed all others at General Motors. He wrote, "… compared to the GM average during a typical period, the pride builders scored 23 percent higher on safety, 10 percent higher on people development, and nine percent higher on a composite of all five measures that compromise GM's plant performance scorecard."[12]

Katzenbach concluded "…Pride is an intrinsic, deeply seated human emotion. It's the one thing that drives performance in the workplace in a number of ways, from creating and delivering a great product or service to winning a colleague's respect."

Author Theodore Kinni agrees. He writes about General Motors' decision to close down an auto plant in 1991 due to lack of profit. The manager told his workers there was no option to save the plant but they *could* make that decision look stupid. With nothing to gain, they began building cars with such excellence, dealers began to request them. In three years, GM chose not to close down the plant after all. The employees made them-selves too valuable to lose. The report was called, *"Pride Goeth Before Profit."*[13]

The fact is, taking pride and owning your work makes you more valuable.

BECOMING A MVP

Over the years, I have hired hundreds of interns, apprentices and new full-time team members. Many were just entering their careers. As I reflect on the ones who got my attention; the ones who stood out and made me want to offer them more opportunity and more salary—it was the individuals who took pride in what they did. They "owned" their job, even when they served as a summer intern.

This idea of ownership was never more clearly illustrated than by Willem, a poor young man who lived over a century ago. Willem wanted to be a missionary to the poor and to make known the plight of the poor to wealthy Europeans. It was this passion that brought him to the coalfields of Belgium in 1879. He served the villagers selflessly, helping to save scores of the miners during disasters, nursing them back to health and giving them most of his money. Then one day—it changed. A visiting church official came to town and saw Willem at his church. The official scoffed at how poorly Willem dressed and how he didn't have good food to eat. When asked why, Willem simply said he'd given his clothes and food to the poor in the village. He was scolded for failing to maintain proper standards in the church. Then, Willem was dismissed.

Needless to say, he was devastated. Willem roamed his village wondering how he might salvage his goal for making known the plight of the poor now that he wasn't even allowed to serve them. That's when an idea hit him. Seeing an old miner bending under the weight of a huge sack of coal, Willem fumbled through his pocket to find a pencil and an old tattered envelope. He began to sketch a picture of the poor miner. It was crude, so he tried it over and over again. Beginning that day, Willem captured for the world the torment, the triumph and dignity of the people he loved. He found a new way to "own" his vision for making the plight of the poor known. For though he failed to achieve his mission as a clergyman, he fulfilled it in another way. We all came to know him as a monumental artist: Vincent Willem Van Gogh. (Harvey, 107)

It's the power of owning your work. All kinds of energy, resourcefulness, creativity, focus and passion surface when someone owns a mission, regardless of where they serve. Doors just seem to open…when you're an owner.

REFLECT AND RESPOND

1. Have you seen this *Habitude* (principle) in action? If so, where?

_____

_____

2. What prevents team members from becoming "owners?"

_____

_____

3. What projects have you taken on where you saw energy and ideas surface because you "owned" the project? What happened?

_____

_____

Self Assessment

Consider your own job. List below two areas where you could make improvements, and treat the mission more like an "owner" than a "renter." Then jot down how.

Area One: _____

How could you improve as an "owner":

_____

_____

Area Two: _____

How could you improve as an "owner":

_____

_____

Exercise

For one week, try expanding your concern for the elements that make up your job. Do something every day this week that enables you to better "own" your work:

- Take time to get to know each of your immediate colleagues: family, back-story, goals and interests. Ask questions and show interest in their personal life.

- Scour each page of the company website, getting fully acquainted with the mission and goals. Jot down what you learn and how you can align your work.

- As you enter or leave your work place, look for ways to improve the space: pick up any trash on the ground, tidy up around the office, or wipe down the kitchen.

- Meet with your direct supervisor and ask how you could demonstrate deeper commitment to the company in your actions and attitude.

After a week, evaluate how you acted and how it made you feel. Did you find yourself more invested in the mission of your organization?

Rubber Bands and Workouts

WE'VE HEARD IT FOR YEARS: NO PAIN, NO GAIN. WE BUILD MUSCLE WHEN OUR WORKOUT LIES BETWEEN STRETCHED AND OVERWHELMED. GROWTH REQUIRES TENSION.

General Taylor was cut out for military life. His dad was a colonel in the revolutionary war, and he raised his five sons to be soldiers. Hard working soldiers. One of them became a general while serving in three long wars, working as hard as any before him and finding ways to win. Taylor loved the rigor of military life. He earned national fame while leading his troops in the Mexican War, in February of 1847. Although he was outnumbered four to one, Taylor outmaneuvered the enemy and won.

At 62 years old, however, General Taylor yearned to return to his plantation in Louisiana and retire. He had no regrets for the decades he'd invested in his troops, his career or his country. The old general was just sure his glory days were over and it was time to finish. When he returned home, however, he realized he'd become a national hero. Mail was stacked high on his front porch, congratulating him on his victories. Because the postal system was relatively new, however, many of the letters arrived with "postage due." We don't know quite how many unpaid congratulatory letters Taylor got, but it must have been a bunch, because he instructed the postman to return all that arrived with postage due to the dead-letter office in Washington D.C.

This would have been the end of General Taylor's story, if it weren't for a friend who visited him. He could tell Taylor was de-motivated by his new lifestyle. After winning battles and conquering enemies as a soldier, his current life was unchallenging. So he inquired if Taylor had received a very important letter a few weeks earlier. Taylor smiled saying he'd given up on reading his mail. His friend assured him he'd want to read this letter. It contained a new opportunity. General Taylor had mixed emotions. While he loved his life of leisure, he was growing dissatisfied by it's lack of excitement, adventure and challenge. He wasn't at his best. So, he sent for the letters he'd returned.

Upon their arrival, he read them all until he found the one his friend mentioned. All the hard work of Taylor's career had paid off. A new "battle" awaited. The "dead letter" was from a political convention in Philadelphia, requesting he, Zachery Taylor, run for president of the United States. He did…and won again.

Zachery Taylor illustrates this *Habitude* well. He found a career he loved and poured his life into it. It didn't feel like "work" because he was passionate about strategy, about his troops and about helping them win. His final victory surfaced as a reward for all the years spent on the battlefield. Each step in his career had stretched him, preparing him for his ultimate role as America's president.

No Pain, No Gain

We've all heard the phrase a thousand times—no pain, no gain. It's actually a paraphrase of something Benjamin Franklin said: "Without pain, there is no gain." He recognized that human growth—in any category—comes only at the price of stretching ourselves intellectually, emotionally, physically, socially or spiritually. Scientist Albert Einstein said, "Intellectual growth should commence at birth and cease only at death."

President Calvin Coolidge explained how: "All growth depends on activity. There is no development physically or intellectually without effort, and effort means work." Author Oscar Wilde noted, "Ambition is the germ from which all noble growth proceeds."

This phrase—no pain, no gain—applies not only to gyms or physical fitness centers, but to work and life. Growth is a sign of life…and growth requires stretching. Strength and conditioning trainers remind us, "in order to produce growth, you have to apply a load of stress greater than to what your body or muscles have previously adapted. This additional tension on the muscle helps to cause changes in the chemistry of the muscle, allowing for growth factors that include motor activation and satellite cell activation."[14] It's why muscles grow larger when we lift heavy weights.

We are Like Rubber Bands

In fact, it was a fitness trainer who first explained it to me this way. He said: People are like rubber bands. They really aren't useful until they are stretched. Our muscles don't grow until they are stretched. Strength expert John Leyva writes "… Metabolic stress causes cell swelling around the muscle, which helps to contribute to muscle growth without necessarily increasing the size of the muscle cells."[15]

So what does this look like at work?

It means realizing that work may feel exhausting at first, right out of college. Your "job muscles" must be developed, which may be different than "school muscles." It likely your supervisor hasn't given you an impossible assignment—you just have to get used to the weight. You need more "reps." How does it look on the job?

- IT MEANS YOU NEED TO BRING A "I WILL FIGURE OUT HOW TO DO THIS PROJECT" MINDSET IF AT FIRST YOU DON'T UNDERSTAND IT. YOUR ATTITUDE IS: "WHATEVER IT TAKES."

- IT MEANS YOU CONTINUE TO LABOR WHEN THE GLITZ AND GLAMOUR ARE GONE FROM THE TASK.

- IT MEANS YOU SEE ALL PROJECTS AS CHALLENGES TO MASTER, LIKE WEIGHTS IN A GYM.

- IT MAY MEAN YOU'LL NEED TO LIFT SMALLER WEIGHTS AT FIRST ON THE JOB TO PREPARE YOU FOR THE BIGGER ONES THAT WILL COME LATER.

Everyone has to get use to a new job or career move. I've found it helpful to remember that I must stretch if I am to grow into it. Lifting makes me stronger.

When J.K. Rowling wrote her first *Harry Potter* book, she learned this truth. She was a waitress and on public assistance. While on a train, she determined she wanted to write stories. She continually received rejection letters...by fourteen publishers. Each time, she decided to try again, like picking up a heavy barbell. She'd tweak the story and edit the manuscript if needed. She would heed the advice she was given, believing this was the "no pain, no gain" process of writing. She was finally published, amusingly because the CEO's 8-year-old daughter begged him to publish it. She said later, "Failure meant a stripping away of the inessential."

SADLY, THIS ISN'T THE NORM

It is unfortunate that stories like J. K. Rowling are rare. I believe there's something great inside of every worker that "heavy lifting" brings out. But people just don't like pain or don't believe it will lead to gain on the job. We seek comfort, convenience, and ease. Far too many never really engage their job like a workout. "Currently, just 30% of the U.S. workforce is engaged in their work, and the ratio of engaged to actively disengaged employees is roughly 2-to-1, meaning that the vast majority of U.S. workers (70%) are not reaching their full potential—a problem that has significant implications for the economy and the individual performance of American companies.

"If this doesn't seem like a big deal, think again. Organizations with an average of 9.3 engaged employees for every actively disengaged employee experiences 147% higher earnings per share (EPS) compared with their competition in a 2011-2012 study. Only 22% of U.S. employees are thriving..."[16]

So What are You Lifting this Week?

This may sound cheesy—but when I work on a project I don't really like, I imagine I am lifting weights. It's not fun at the time, but I know I'm developing an internal *job muscle* in the process. I also kept a rubber band on my work desk for years reminding me I must be stretched to be useful. This framework enables me to continue when it's not fun. It helps the hurt. I believe we are at our best when we are on the job, and:

Living Between Stretched and Overwhelmed

Consider the alternative. When you're not being stretched at work, you can become bored, just like a workout that only demands you lift two-pound weights. I tell our team I want them to be serving in their gift areas, but going after tasks that position them between "stretched" (*this task is asking me to push myself*) and "overwhelmed" (*this task is beyond my limits*). Naturally, we all go through times feeling overwhelmed. We should not live in this state constantly. But living in between these two boundaries pushes us to improve, like a good trainer in a gym.

I believe our growth at work should focus on two areas:

1. Our strengths: The majority of the tasks fit into your personal gift areas.

2. Our needs: The rest should focus on areas we must grow in to succeed.

I love the story of Jia Jiang, a social entrepreneur from China. He'd dreamed of leading a start-up company, after working at a Fortune 500 company for six years. He was too comfortable and knew it was time to take a risk. He felt if he took this next career step, he'd have to become comfortable with rejection. He was afraid. He hated rejection. So, he initiated something he called "rejection therapy."

Rejection therapy meant that he would come up with all kinds of crazy requests he would make of people, knowing that they would reject it, thus desensitizing him to the fear of rejection. He called it "100 Days of Rejection." Like lifting weights, he'd get used to it. The experiment was hilarious. Mr. Jiang traveled around to neighborhoods, stores and restaurants asking for things like:

1. Will you let me have a "hamburger refill" at a fast food restaurant?
2. Can I serve as a live mannequin for Abercrombie and Fitch?
3. Would you let me give a weather forecast on live TV?
4. Can I make an announcement on a Southwest flight?
5. Would you allow me to play soccer in your backyard? (He got a "yes"!)

Making these crazy requests did the trick. After asking dozens of people for outrageous wishes (and getting some to say yes), Jia Jiang won his battle over fear of rejection. But it was like a workout. He lifted the weights of "fear" until he was not overwhelmed. He said later, "The only things standing between me and my dream…is me."[17]

Reflect and Respond

1. Why is it so rare for employees to approach their work like a workout?

_____

_____

2. Do you currently perform a task that is boring to you? What could you do to make it more challenging and more engaging?

_____

_____

3. What projects are you working on that feel a little like weight lifting? Have you seen improvement? (You've demonstrated the ability to lift heavier weights.)

_____

_____

Self Assessment

Reflect on two common tasks you perform in your work. Then, evaluate each of them based on the scale below. Place a mark where you see yourself as you serve:

Task One: _____

Light Lifting   Heavy Lifting
I --- I
   Bored   Comfortable   Stretched   Overwhelmed

Task Two: _____

Light Lifting   Heavy Lifting
I --- I
   Bored   Comfortable   Stretched   Overwhelmed

Exercise

Choose one of the tasks you listed above, and give yourself a workout. It's best to select a task where you feel you're lingering between bored and comfortable. Then, meet with your supervisor and discuss how you could stretch yourself while performing that job. What could you do to improve your results? How could you make the task better for the next person who takes it on? What could you add or tweak to take production to a higher level? Then, take those steps for a week. Discuss it with a group when you're finished.

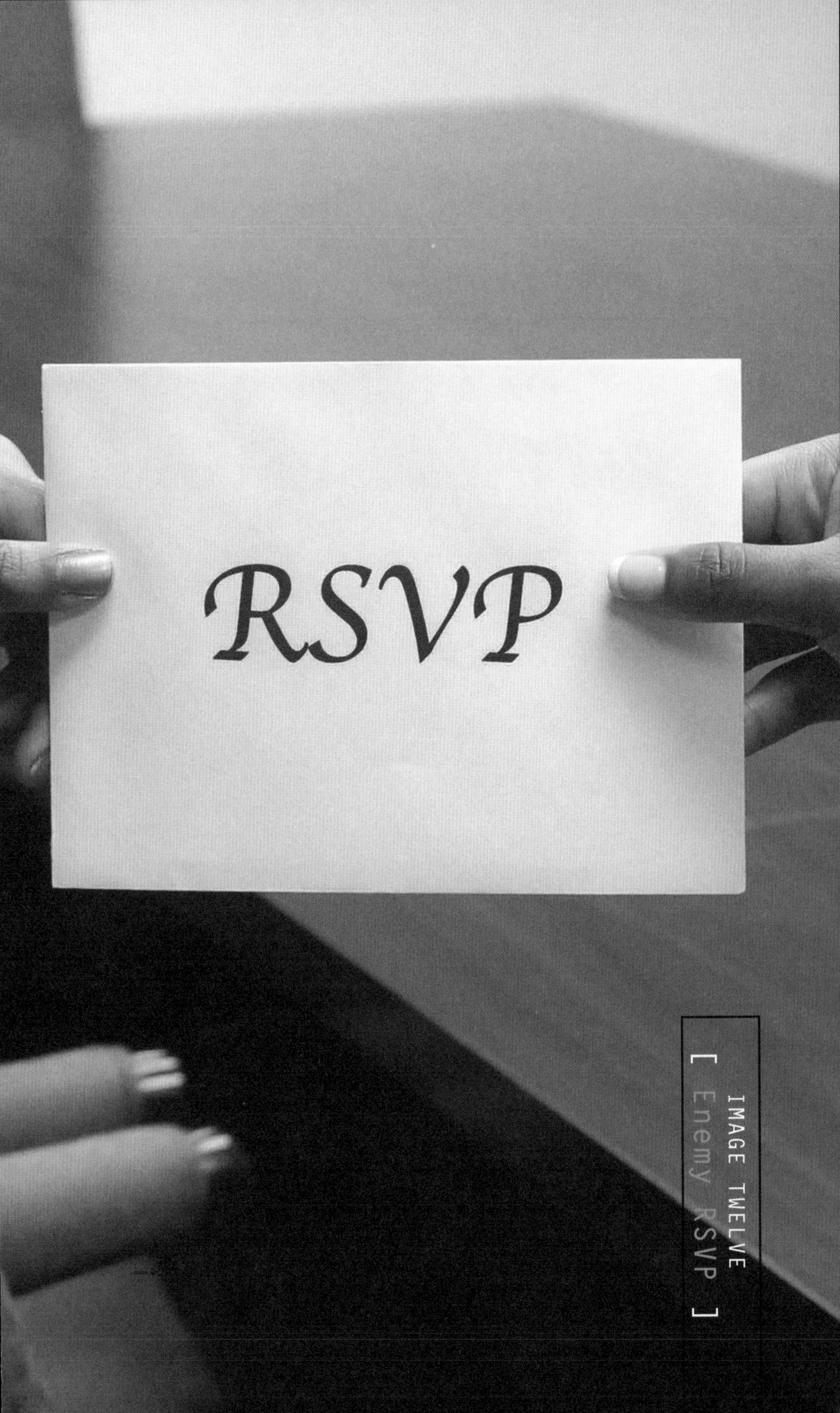

IMAGE TWELVE [Enemy RSVP]

RSVP

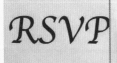

Enemy RSVP

FRIENDS MAY COME AND GO, BUT ENEMIES ACCUMULATE. KEEPING SCORE INVITES
ANTAGONISTS ON THE JOB. IT PUTS OTHERS IN AN ADVERSARIAL POSITION TO
MONITOR PERFORMANCE. ENTITLEMENT AND GRACE CANNOT CO-EXIST.

There's an old legend about two brothers who lived next door to each other for
years. At one point, they had an argument that turned into a major falling out.
Neither of them spoke to the other for years. Instead, they each silently did things
out of spite, just to annoy the other. One would throw loud parties late into the
night. In response, the other would cut down a tree, allowing the branches to fall
on his brother's property.

Finally one brother decided he'd make a statement by creating a small river between
their two properties. It would be a visual sign of the separation they felt between
each other. It was at that point the second brother knew he had to make a similar
statement in reply. After all, they were enemies. One day, a carpenter came by to
ask if he needed any work done on his home. The second brother smiled, knowing
this was his chance to retaliate. He told the carpenter to get some wood and
build a wall on the property line, so he'd never have to see that stupid river. The
carpenter agreed, purchased the wood and asked if his work could be a surprise to
the buyer, suggesting he take a short trip while the carpenter did his construction.
The brother agreed.

When he returned days later, the man noticed his alienated brother was on his
doorstep. Expecting a fight, he approached him, but instead his brother embraced
him, and with tears in his eyes, he apologized for how childish he'd been over the
years. It seemed the wall had done the trick. But when the man went to see what
the carpenter had built, he realized what had happened to resolve the conflict.
There was no wall at all. The carpenter had built a bridge from one property to
the other.

When both men asked if the carpenter could stay for a meal, he replied, "I'm sorry,
but I can't stay. I've got too many other bridges I need to build."

While this legend may seem a bit cheesy, it's been around for years because it remains relevant in every generation. Far too often, people allow rifts or disagreements to mount between them. Like the brothers, both parties begin doing and saying things that further the separation. The dispute turns into the "Hatfields and the McCoys." Sadly, grown adults often need a third party, like the carpenter, to help build a bridge.

It Happens All the Time

Believe it or not, the easiest place for this to happen is the workplace. Think about it. You usually don't get to choose who you work alongside. They get hired. They may be different; they may have obnoxious habits or personalities and on top of that possess poor people skills. The easiest reaction to this type of person is to alienate yourself from them; to allow petty differences to be a wall further separating you from them.

Years ago, I learned an important reality from a mentor. Simply put, it goes like this:

> *"Friends may come and go, but enemies accumulate."*

It's true. The reason is—we let it happen. Instead of making things right when disputes surface, we keep score. We start a mental "filing cabinet" storing away all the memories (like files) of the negative things the other person has said or done. Soon, you have huge sets of files stored up that you never really discard. It just gets bigger and bigger. They probably have a file on you as well. One day when one of you leaves the job, instead of making things right, you both carry these files with you, like extra weight. Then, if you ever see that person in a restaurant or a store, it's awkward. You tend to avoid them, or at best, put on a fake smile and act like you are glad to see them.

This is ultimate immaturity.

So, here's what I suggest instead. Take initiative to meet. Ask for an RSVP. Just like you request an RSVP when you throw a party for friends, seeking a response from invitees about their intentions, I believe its healthy to extend an invitation to people who feel alienated, and seek an RSVP. Initiate a conversation. Don't just let relationships hang or drift. Express an "invitation" for the purpose of making things right between you. Even though you may never be "BFFs", it's always wise to at least restore a connection with them. Why? Because friends come and go—but enemies accumulate.

The fact is, we live in a mobile and disposable society. It is easier to "unfriend" a person on Facebook or delete them from our contacts, than to actually make things right. We are not good at apologizing or resolving conflict—so we just avoid the whole thing.

This makes for a poor and unhealthy work culture. Tons of sideways energy is spent on negative emotions instead of achieving the mission of the company. It's wasted human energy. It's a distraction. Believe it or not, it harms both you and the team. Some sources indicate that Human Resource managers spend between 25-60 percent of their time resolving employee conflict.[18] A University of North Carolina study revealed that over half of workers said anxiety about a past or current conflict with a co-worker cost them time while on the job. More than a quarter said they are less productive because they spent time trying to avoid a confrontation with a colleague. Sadly, even violent confrontations are increasing. A Society of Human Resource Management study found that more than half of workers said a violent act had occurred at their workplace.[19]

Case in point. Leigh came across confident and skillful at her job interview. When she was hired, her team members realized it was a façade. Deep down, she was insecure and always kept score, comparing herself to teammates. When a colleague was praised or promoted, she grew jealous and began talking trash about him. In fact, if anything happened that didn't somehow benefit her, she gossiped about those who did benefit. It became clear she felt entitled to special perks, which created all kinds of negative relationships with team members. Sadly, no one confronted her, knowing that they'd become the victims of her wrath. Her supervisor finally fired her when Leigh's anger surfaced, resulting in screaming at everyone who crossed her. In the end, she had created dissension between colleagues and decreased productivity by more than 50 percent. One bad apple spoiled the bunch.

So How Do We Send a RSVP?

We'll all run into conflict sooner or later. This is why everyone must develop effective conflict resolution skills. They're an essential component of a being a good team member. Not only does unresolved conflict result in loss of productivity, it stifles creativity, and erects barriers to cooperation and collaboration. When teams practice good conflict resolution skills, they tend to stay together longer. The challenge lies in how we choose to deal with conflict. Concealed, avoided or otherwise ignored, conflict will likely fester only to grow into resentment.

The root of most conflict is either born out of poor communication or the inability to control one's emotions. This is why emotional intelligence during conflict is such a valuable skill set. Former First Lady Barbara Bush put it this way, "Never lose sight of the fact that the most important yardstick of your success will be how you treat other people: your family, friends, coworkers, and even strangers you meet along the way."

So in our office, we constantly work on this principle. Although we have a variety of personalities and styles, just like your workplace does, we follow these principles:

1. Keep short accounts. When a disagreement rises, seek to resolve it quickly.

2. Don't talk about people, talk to them. Gossip divides. Conversation unites.

3. People are down on what they're not up on. Continually communicate.

4. Take initiative. Hostility grows when things are left simmering and unsaid.

5. Technical skills without soft skills eventually sabotage the team. Team members need to be good at both relationships and results.

It's imperative you keep negative "stuff" from piling up. Frustrations. Disappointments. Feeling entitled to something you didn't get. All these foster dreadful opinions about people we work alongside. The easiest thing to do is to allow animosity to surface.

When facing disagreements at work...

1. Expect conflict. It's normal when working together.

2. Find a mediator if necessary. If the conflict is emotional invite a third party.

3. Be open to compromise. Both parties may need to give in a little.

4. Repeat what you heard them say. This helps you relay understanding.

5. Don't personalize or internalize disagreements. You can disagree agreeably.

6. Use professional language. Don't hit below the belt with ugly words.

7. Let everyone speak. Folks don't need to get their way; they do need to be heard.

8. Choose your battles. Be sure the topic is worth your time and energy.

Abraham Lincoln mastered this *Habitude*. While president, he was despised by many of his own cabinet, but he worked to harmonize with each one. After he died, staff found a desk drawer in the oval office filled with angry letters he'd written in reaction to these difficult people. He chose to write them, but never send them. Instead, he sent RSVP's. Edwin Stanton, his Secretary of War, was especially cruel to Lincoln. Stanton called Lincoln an ape, ridiculing how he handled his presidency. One day, a staff member asked Mr. Lincoln what he thought of Mr. Stanton. Lincoln smiled and replied he felt Stanton was a brilliant leader and strategist. The staff member was shocked and asked if Lincoln knew what Stanton had said about him. The president smiled again and said, "Yes I do. But you didn't ask his opinion of me. You asked what I thought of him."

Reflect and Respond

1. Practicing this *Habitude* is hard for most people. What makes it so hard?

_____

_____

2. What have you noticed people tend to do when facing conflict?

_____

_____

Self Assessment

Are there any relationships at work that you've allowed to sour or become unhealthy? Place a number below (1 - 4) indicating your most likely response when this happens:

- Avoid them altogether _____
- Neglect to face the issue but keep score on them _____
- Go to your supervisor to seek input or intervention _____
- Seek them out to make the relationship right _____

Exercise

When you need to confront or clarify a disagreement, I suggest the steps from Josh Isenhardt, called:
Navigating Confrontation: Arriving at WE from YOU against ME [20]:

1. Define Your Goal

   - What do you want? (Is it realistic? Is it reasonable?)

   - What do you NOT want? (What could you lose?)

2. Determine Your Point Of View

   - OBSERVE: "What did I see and hear?"

   - BELIEVE: "What do I believe about what I saw and heard?"

   - EMOTE: "How did what I believe make me feel?"

   - DO: "How did I respond?"

3. Decide On Your Approach

- Who

- When

- Where

4. Dialogue With Humility

- Share Your Point Of View

- Observations and Beliefs

- Attitudes and Emotions

- Actions

5. Discover Their Point Of View

- Add to your facts

- Adjust your beliefs

- Own your actions

6. Develop a Plan

- Who does what by when?

- How will we know when it's completed?

IMAGE THIRTEEN
[Faithful and Fruitful]

Faithful and Fruitful

TO BE FAITHFUL IS GOOD. TO BE FRUITFUL IS NECESSARY. THE GOAL OF WORK IS NOT BUSYNESS, BUT RESULTS. ACTIVITY ISN'T ACCOMPLISHMENT. LABOR TO ADD VALUE.

Benjamin Franklin was one of our most significant Founding Fathers. You learned about him in your U.S. history class, right? He was a statesman, ambassador, inventor, politician, writer, printer, and his face is on our one hundred dollar bill. Not bad for a guy who never became president, right?

So what made him so successful? So productive? So memorable?

The answer to this question could make you valuable to your workplace. Let's review his story. Young Ben's parents didn't have much money. They could only afford to keep him in school until he turned ten. After that, his growth was up to him. Although he left school, he did not stop learning. He was motivated by a thirst for knowledge and taught himself through extensive reading. What's more, his reading always led to action. Benjamin believed the best way to really learn something was to do it. Practice it. Experiment until you master it and see results.

His chief secret to success was that he worked backward from his goal. He would start with a problem that needed solving. Then, he'd envision the result he desperately wanted, and beginning with the end in mind, he'd labor until he got his result. No doubt, the result sometimes became a discovery he did not expect. But he was driven by productivity not activity. This is key. He was all about one big idea: solve problems that will serve people.

He went on to invent the lightning rod, bifocals, the U.S. public (social) library, the urinary catheter, swim fins, the odometer, American political cartoons, the glass harmonica, the method to harness electricity, the long-arm reaching device, the Franklin stove…and so many more items. Despite the fact that he was never a U.S. president, he advised them, both at home and abroad. He was all about results.

Activity is Not Accomplishment

This is the big idea behind the *Habitude, Faithful or Fruitful*. To faithfully execute routine tasks is very important. It's crucial to remember, however, that activity does not equal accomplishment. Your organization does not pay you to stay busy but to be productive. To get results. To achieve something at the end of the day. They want the hours you put in to actually bear fruit.

Let me ask you a question. Are you working to *keep busy* or to *make better*? Busyness is not always better-ness. Every team member must figure out their supervisor's scorecard…then, work backward from that scorecard if they want to succeed.

Here's why I underscore this simple principle. Often, a new employee enters their job feeling a little intimidated. They wonder: *Can I make it here? Will they like me? Will I get noticed or will I get lost in the crowd?* This feeling of inadequacy can often lead a new team member to work simply to "not lose" rather than to "win" on the job. They begin hoping to stay busy, keep their nose clean and not mess up. They play defense rather than offense. They just don't want to fail. Sadly, this mindset prevents them from the very thing they desire—to stand out and make progress in their career. Instead of standing out, they merely blend in. They may be "faithful" but not "fruitful."

Turning Things Around

Over the years, we have seen several young team members fear taking risks or merely misunderstand the goal for their work. They slip into the trap of "doing time" almost like they were in prison. They think: *If I just look busy, all will be well.* Sadly, those people never stay very long on our team. Our leaders have had to meet with such young team members and help them see: faithfulness is not fruitfulness. Then, we'd help them attack their work like Ben Franklin did:

- First, **fully understand the problem that needs to be solved.**

- Second, **envision what solutions would best serve the people involved.**

- Third, **with that target in mind, work backward from the goal.**

In the early 1970s, Dr. Judah Folkman worked alongside other medical professionals. While they plodded away at the assigned tasks, he was consumed with the problem of cancer. Believing there had to be a solution, this ignited him to go beyond clocking hours in a lab. He came up with an idea for cancer research, but scientists rejected it since it didn't fit their current paradigm. Over and over they told him, "You're studying dirt." Although he was constantly criticized, he worked relentlessly for twenty years. He believed his work could stop the growth of tumors. By the early 1980s, Folkman and his colleagues discovered the first angiogenesis inhibitors. This "fruit" drove him and his team to continue. In the end, Dr. Folkman's work now benefits more than 100,000 cancer patients today. Certainly, he had to be faithful at his work—but it was the fruit at the end that drove him.

This is often the difference between a typical employee and an entrepreneur. Many employees begin their job each day believing the goal is to show up on time at work, do the projects in front of them, and clock out at the end of the workday. Entrepreneurs, on the other hand, know they won't eat unless they get results; unless they sell a product or a service. Unless they invent or create something. Why? Because they are in a start-up. They have to produce. If they don't, results won't happen. This is the spirit with which I wish every person approached their career. John D. Rockefeller once said, "I believe in the dignity of labor, whether with head or hand; that the world owes no man a living but that it owes every man an opportunity to make a living."

In fact, research demonstrates that seeing the fruit of your labor actually motivates. In a study conducted at Harvard University, behavioral economist, Dan Ariely asked participants to build characters from Lego's Bionicles series. But while one group's creations were stored under the table, to be disassembled at the end of the experiment, the other group's Legos were disassembled as soon as they'd been built. What did they discover? The first group made 11 Bionicles, on average, while the second group made only seven before they quit. Ariely noted that "even though there wasn't huge meaning at stake, seeing the results of their labor for even a short time was enough to dramatically improve performance…"

Next, Ariely gave study participants a piece of paper filled with random letters and asked them to find pairs of identical letters. Each round, they were offered less money than the previous round. People in the first group wrote their names on their sheets and handed them to the experimenter, who looked it over and said "Uh huh" before putting it in a pile. People in the second group didn't write down their names, and the experimenter put their sheets in a pile without looking at them. People in the third group had their work shredded immediately upon completion. Again, it was a simple exercise without much meaning. What the experimenters found, however, enlightens us to understand the power of "results" in our work. People whose work was shredded needed twice as much money as those whose work was acknowledged in order to keep doing the task. People in the second group, whose work was saved but ignored, needed almost as much money as people whose work was shredded.[20]

What Motivates Us to Work?

I believe each of us perform better when we see the fruit of our labor. Further, I believe we will be more highly motivated when we believe our work actually matters. I will never forget hearing about a college student who had participated in the famous Rose Bowl Parade every January 1st. He was interviewed on TV his senior year after wining awards all four years for his school's float. When he was asked if he enjoyed it, he quickly smiled and said it was the highlight of his school year, every year. When he was asked if he could imagine making a career out of building floats like the ones he'd built for the Rose Bowl—he immediately said no. When questioned why, his response was insightful. He replied, "Because I cannot imagine investing so much of myself into a project that will be thrown into the garbage a week later."

We tend to work more passionately when we believe our work is important and it lasts. It solves problems that serve people. Motivation rises when we see the outcomes of our work. I believe it's wise to do a gut check on our work every week. Is it all about busyness or better-ness? Is it to be faithful or fruitful?

Anthony Burgess passed away in November of 1993. He died as a novelist, the author of *A Clockwork Orange*. His story is a picture of this *Habitude*. His career went from faithful to fruitful in midlife. When he was 40, he learned he only had a year to live. Doctors found a brain tumor that was terminal. Burgess was broke and had nothing to leave his wife when he died. While he worked during his life, that's all he did. His work didn't add anything of significant value, and he did not really invest himself in his work. At least, until he was shaken up with the news of his tumor. Because he had but a short time to live, he decided to take the opportunity to do something he'd always wanted: to write. He wrote five and half novels in one year. Amazingly, he did not die. His cancer went into remission and then disappeared. From then on, he kept writing, adding passion to his labor, and wrote more than seventy books in his lifetime. He died at 76 both successful and satisfied.

That's what I call fruitful.

REFLECT AND RESPOND

1. Have you seen anyone fall into the trap of "busyness", focusing on the routine instead of the result? Have you ever done this?

_____

_____

2. What keeps people from working with the end in mind?

_____

_____

3. What tasks are most fulfilling to you? Do these also produce the most results?

_____

_____

SELF ASSESSMENT

Consider your own job again. What tasks have you slipped into "faithful" mode instead of "fruitful" mode? In other words, where have you lost sight of the real goal? Then, jot down why you believe you've drifted into "auto pilot":

Task One: _____

Why have you slipped into auto-pilot?

_____

_____

Task Two: _____

Why have you slipped into auto-pilot?

_____

_____

Exercise

List every one of the routine tasks you do on your job on any given week. Then, next to each one, jot down one way—one method you could use—to improve the results of your work. Try working with the end in mind:

- What problem are you trying to solve?

- What solution best serves the people involved?

- With your target in mind, work backward to get results.

Evaluate yourself. Does working in view of the goal, to bear the greatest fruit, help at all? How does starting with the problem you hope to solve help you work smarter?

Francis Bacon wrote: *"It's not what we eat but digest that makes us strong; not what we gain but save that makes us rich; not what we read but remember that makes us learned; not what we profess but practice that gives us integrity."*

The content below makes up a simple list of suggestions for how to approach work situations that may be a bit controversial. Every organization is different, so keep in mind, these are only suggestions. I realize some of them will seem conservative or old-fashioned. It's because I'd rather you not assume too much on the job, and allow your supervisor to communicate a more relaxed set of rules.

TATTOOS

If you have one, it's best to keep it out of sight. I still know many companies that frown on tattoos in the workplace since they unwittingly communicate a message that is less than professional. Some just won't hire a candidate who has a visible one on the neck, arm or leg. If you have one, ask about the policy on them before sporting it.

PIERCINGS

Like tattoos, a nose, eyebrow or lip piercing communicates something less than professional. Believe it or not, piercings and tattoos scream the message: "I'm figuring out who I am, and suspect my identity is drawn from the outside, not within." I suggest you ask about these during the interview. You may have hide it or lose it.

CELL PHONES

As a rule, it's best not to take your phone to a meeting unless everyone does. Consider the message it sends to others when you check your cell phone. You're basically signaling: *There are other people more important than the ones in the room with me.* If you take a phone, computer or tablet to a meeting, use it for note taking and let people know what you're doing.

HAIR COLOR

I would not suggest you take a job interview or a job wearing an unnatural hair color on top of your head. Why? It still screams adolescence. Immaturity. I know that sounds old-fashioned, but that's the message it sends. Use natural hair color and later ask about policies on purple or pink, etc. For many, it still screams you're superficial. Don't forget, every choice you make builds your personal brand.

CLOTHES AND SHOES

Usually, you can tell right away the proper dress code for a workplace. Many today are business-casual, while others lie on both extremes—business formal or extreme casual. I suggest you stand out through your job performance not your attire. To be safe, a good rule of thumb is to match or dress one notch higher than the code.

Ear Buds and Music

If you work out in an open space, it often helps to wear ear buds and listen to music while you work to prevent getting distracted by those near you. However, always ask your supervisor about this—as they may interpret it as a distraction itself from the job. If you want to wear them, tell your colleagues it's for the purpose of staying focused.

Language

Most businesses today prefer warm but professional language. This means it's better not to swear on the job (using four-letter words). Beyond that, I suggest you remove over-used words from your vocabulary. For example, do you use the word "like" as a verbal tic? *I mean, like, do you insert it in, like, randomly into, like, your conversation?*

Eliminate this from your vocabulary. It screams you're unready for professional work.

Gum and Food

I would start the job *not* assuming you can chew gum or eat food while working. Then, observe those in management. If you want to move up, act like those who are above you. There's nothing wrong with gum, but it's often a signal of informality and youth. Be sure that's the signal you want to send.

Familiarity with Management

Always begin using formal greetings with a boss; then only use their first names when they insist. When addressing someone who is old enough to be your parent, many still prefer to be addressed with a proper title. Once you become familiar with them, that's when it may be appropriate to call them by their first name. Follow their lead.

Texting and Social Media

It is better to assume you should not be using social media for personal reasons on the job—Instagram, Facebook, Snapchat or even texting personal messages. You've exchanged your time for money—your boss owns your time on the job. If you have to use social media, wait for breaks or lunchtime.

Noise

If you have a flamboyant personality, you'll want to be careful about making too much noise on phone calls or in conversations. Always, always think of others and how your voice may invade their work. If you remain humble and thoughtful you'll make good decisions. In fact, if you're thoughtful of others, you'll find they often return the favor.

IDENTITY

Remember—you are building your personal brand with every decision you make: what you wear, what you say, what you post, what you work on, how you talk about others, what you value, how you think and how well you perform. Remembering this can work as a fantastic barometer on your style at work. Always ask yourself: *If you were the boss, would you hire YOU?*

A Story to End on...

Let me leave you with a quick story that says it all. A teenager entered a convenience store and promptly dialed a number on the payphone. The store manager overheard the following conversation from the young man:

Teen: "Lady, I'm interested in a job. I heard you were looking for someone to oversee your shipping room. Is that job still available?"

Woman: (at the other end of the phone): "I already have someone in that position."

Boy: "Ma'am, I'll bet I'm less expensive than the person who does it now."

Woman: "I'm very satisfied with the person who presently does shipping for us."

Boy: (with more perseverance): "You don't understand. I will work hard, keep a great attitude and I'm always punctual. I'll sweep the floor, organize the shelves, clean the equipment and even have the shipments ready early every day."

Woman: "Wow. You sound amazing—but I already have someone I'm totally satisfied with who does all those things. I appreciate it, but no, thanks."

With a smile on his face, the teen hung up the phone. The store manager, who was listening to all this, walked over to the boy.

Manager: "Son...I couldn't help but overhear your call. I like your attitude; I like that work ethic you described and would like to offer you a job."

Boy: "No thanks."

Store Owner: "But weren't you just pleading for a job?"

Boy: "No Sir, I don't need a new job. I was just checking my performance at the job I already have."

Question: Could you make this phone call and get the same response?

[End Notes]

1. Rice, Condoleeza and Klein, Joel, U.S. Education Reform and National Security, March 2012, http://www.cfr.org/united-states/us-education-reform-national-security/p27618.

2. Levit, Alexandria, "They Don't Teach Corporate in College," and Siverberg, Bret, "Paying your dues in the workplace" Dues.

3. http://www.sagepub.com/upm-data/7668_Chapter_1.pdf

4. (Source: "How to Get Disengaged Employees to go the Extra Mile" by Bruna Martinuzzi; Link)

5. Source: "Employee Motivation: Theory and practice"; Link 2

6. http://phys.org/news/2013-06-world-powerful-microscope-ready.html

7. http://phys.org/news/2013-06-world-powerful-microscope-ready.html#jCp

8. Source: "On Making Judgments and Being Judgmental" by Gregg Henriques; Judgmental)

9. Matthew 7:5

10. "Employee Distrust is Pervasive in U.S. Workforce" APA Survey; 2014 https://www.apa.org/news/press/releases/2014/04/employee-distrust.aspx

11. "The Speed of Trust: The One Thing that Changes Everything," Stephen M.R. Covey / Link 1

12. "Instilling Pride: The Primary Motivator of Peak Performance" by Jon Katzenbach; Pride 2)

13. "Pride Goeth Before Profit" by Theodore Kinni; Pride)

14. Source: "How Do Muscles? The Science of Muscle Growth" by John Leyva; Muscles)

15. Ibid

16. "State of the American Workplace: Employee Engagement Insights for U.S. Business Leaders"; Study)

17. Rejection Therapy Experiment: http://www.fearbuster.com/100-days-of-rejection-therapy/

18. [source: Zupek].

19. Ibid

20. http://www.simple-message.com/

21. "What motivates us to work? 7 fascinating studies that give insights" by Jessica Gross; Studies)

Acknowledgements

This book, like most of the Habitudes series, was a team effort. The entire Growing Leaders team was involved, providing input on the concepts. I want to especially thank Constantina Kokenes who researched for each chapter, finding "nuggets" to illustrate the principles. I am forever grateful, Connie. In addition, I am grateful to Alyson Carroll who did the editing. Alyson—you excel with words. I also want to thank Jim Woodard who did the layout and gathered the images. Jim—you never cease to amaze me. You never fail to come through. I also want to thank Andrea Callicott who protected my weekly writing days. And we couldn't have done this project without our main photographer Levi Woodard. Levi—you went beyond the call of duty. Finally, I must thank Holly Moore who always proofs these resources to insure they are everything they were meant to be. She leads our team in practicing these habits and attitudes.

Tim Elmore

[Notes]

[Notes]

[Notes]

Enjoy Habitudes?

Help us bring these lessons to students who can't afford them.

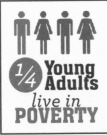

1/4 Young Adults *live in* **POVERTY**

8/10 Young Adults *plan to* **MOVE HOME** *after College*

In both urban and rural environments, **students are sheltered** *within a 9-mile radius of their home,* **shielded from experiences** *that involve risk or failure.* **This leads to delayed maturity.**

All over the country and in developing nations around the world, there are students who are not equipped to lead themselves (or others) into the next steps of their lives. What's worse, their schools can't afford leadership development materials to help them mature into the best versions of themselves.

We want to change that. We want to help students broaden their vision, take bigger risks, think bigger thoughts, and pursue bigger goals.

To do this, we created **The Growing Leaders Initiative**, to provide *Habitudes* in schools and youth non-profit organizations that cannot afford to purchase programs for their students. Thanks to donor support, grants are available for qualified applicants.

To apply or donate, visit
www.TheGrowingLeadersInitiative.com.

The **GROWING LEADERS** Initiative

Contributing Photographers

We would like to thank the photographers

who contributed to the images that anchored

each of these Habitude images:

Jessica Kirste - Jessica Kirste Photography

Levi Woodard - Woodard Photography